Additional Practice and Skills Workbook

Grade 8

Glenda Lappan
James T. Fey
William M. Fitzgerald
Susan Friel
Elizabeth Difanis Phillips

Boston, Massachusetts
Upper Saddle River, New Jersey

***Connected Mathematics*™ Project was developed at Michigan State University with financial support from the Michigan State University Office of the Provost, Computing and Technology, and the College of Natural Science.**

Connected Mathematics™ is based upon work supported by the National Science Foundation under Grant No. MDR 9150217 and Grant No. ESI 9986372. Opinions expressed are those of the authors and not necessarily those of the Foundation.

The Michigan State University authors and administration have agreed that all MSU royalties arising from this publication will be devoted to purposes supported by the Department of Mathematics and the MSU Mathematics Enrichment Fund.

Acknowledgments The people who made up the ***Connected Mathematics 2*** team—representing editorial, editorial services, design services, and production services—are listed below. Bold type denotes core team members.

Leora Adler, Judith Buice, Kerry Cashman, Patrick Culleton, Sheila DeFazio, Katie Hallahan, Richard Heater, **Barbara Holllingdale, Jayne Holman,** Karen Holtzman, **Etta Jacobs,** Christine Lee, Carolyn Lock, Catherine Maglio, **Dotti Marshall,** Rich McMahon, Eve Melnechuk, Terri Mitchell, **Marsha Novak,** Irene Rubin, Donna Russo, Robin Samper, Siri Schwartzman, **Nancy Smith,** Emily Soltanoff, **Mark Tricca,** Paula Vergith, Roberta Warshaw, Helen Young.

ISBN 0-13-165616-3
1 2 3 4 5 6 7 8 9 10 09 08 07 06 05

Table of Contents

Kaleidoscopes, Hubcaps, and Mirrors

Say It With Symbols

The Shapes of Algebra

Samples and Populations

Name ______________________ Date __________ Class __________

Additional Practice

1. Toothpicks were used to make the pattern below.

1st 2nd 3rd 4th

a. How many toothpicks will be in the 5th figure? In the 6th figure?

b. Write an equation for the number of toothpicks t needed to make the nth figure.

c. Identify and describe the figure in this pattern that can be made with exactly 100 toothpicks.

d. Describe the pattern in words.

e. Make a graph of the data.

f. Is the pattern linear or not linear? Explain.

2. Toothpicks were used to make the pattern below.

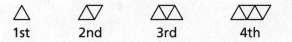

1st 2nd 3rd 4th

a. How many toothpicks will be in the 5th figure? In the 6th figure?

b. Write an equation for the number of toothpicks t needed to make the nth figure.

Additional Practice *(continued)*

c. Identify and describe the figure in this pattern that can be made with exactly 61 toothpicks.

d. Describe the pattern in words.

e. Make a graph of the data.

f. Is the pattern linear or not linear? Explain.

3. Square tiles were used to make the pattern below.

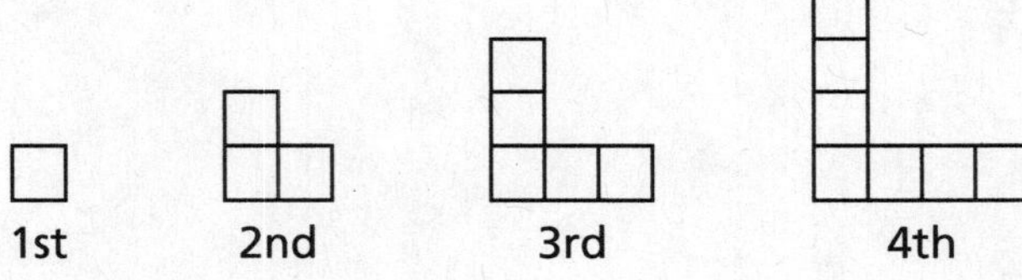

a. How many tiles will be in the 5th figure? In the 6th figure?

b. Write an equation for the number of tiles t needed to make the nth figure.

c. Identify and describe the figure in this pattern that can be made with exactly 25 tiles.

d. Describe the pattern in words.

Name ______________________ Date ____________ Class ____________

Additional Practice (continued)

e. Make a graph of the data.

f. Is the pattern linear or not linear? Explain.

4. Square tiles were used to make the pattern below.

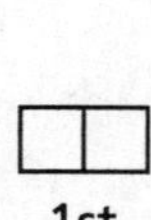
1st

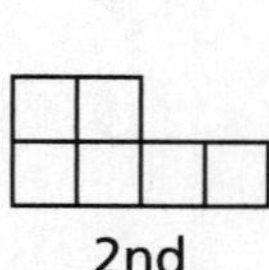
2nd

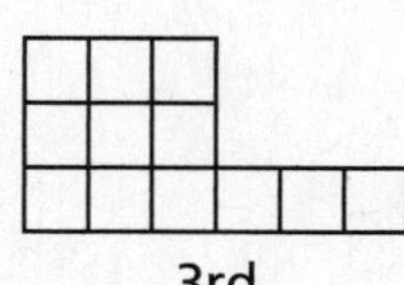
3rd

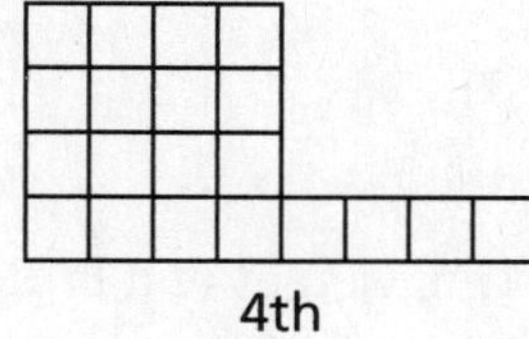
4th

a. How many tiles will be in the 5th figure? In the 6th figure?

b. Write an equation for the number of tiles t needed to make the nth figure.

c. Identify and describe the figure in this pattern that can be made with exactly 420 tiles.

d. Describe the pattern in words.

e. Make a graph of the data.

f. Is the pattern linear or not linear? Explain.

Name ______________________ Date ____________ Class ____________

Additional Practice *(continued)*

5. a. Make a graph of the data. Draw a line to show the trend and write an equation for the line. This group used construction paper for their bridges.

Bridge-Thickness Data

Thickness (layers)	1	2	3	4	5	6
Breaking Weight (pennies)	24	38	50	67	78	93

b. Predict the breaking weight of a bridge made from 14 layers of construction paper.

6. a. Complete the table using the graph:

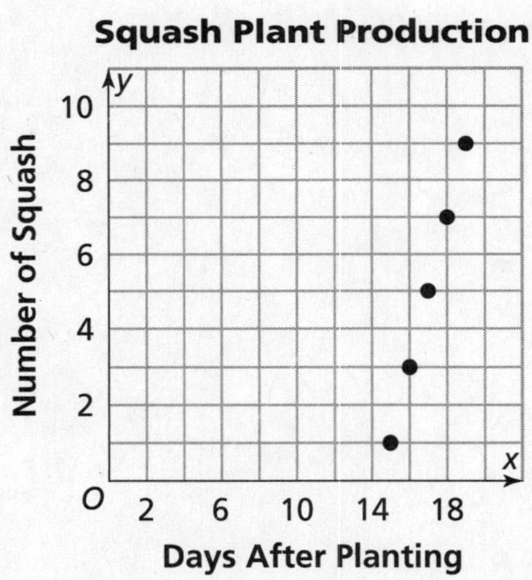

Day	15	16	17	18	19
Total Number of Squash					

b. If the pattern continues, what is the total number of squash that would be produced by day 22? By day 26?

c. Describe the pattern in words. What can you say about the number of squash produced each day?

d. Describe the pattern with an equation. What does the coefficient of x mean in this situation?

7. Betty went to the store to buy pepper. There were three different jars on the shelf:

1 ounce jar costs $0.65, *4 ounce jar costs $1.40,* *8 ounce jar costs $2.40*

a. Make a table and draw a graph for these data.

b. Predict the cost of 2 ounces, 3 ounces, and 6 ounces.

c. Describe the pattern in words. What can you say about the cost of a jar? What can you say about the cost of an ounce of pepper alone?

d. Describe the pattern with an equation. What information do the variables and numbers represent?

Name ______________________________ Date ____________ Class ____________

Skill: Patterns and Predictions

Complete each table.

1.

Time (h)	1	2	3	4	7
Distance cycled (mi)	8	16	24	32	

2.

Time (min)	1	2	3	4	7
Distance from surface of water (yd)	−3	−2	−1	0	

For Exercises 3–4, find the values of the missing entries in each table.

3.

m	4	6		10
n	24	26	28	

4.

p		6	10	14
q	1	13	25	

5. A pattern of squares is shown. 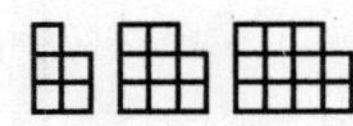

a. Sketch the 4th and 5th figure in this pattern.

b. Make a table comparing the figure number to the number of squares. Write an expression for the number of squares in the nth figure.

Name ________________________________ Date __________ Class __________

Skill: Patterns and Predictions *(continued)*

Make a table for each function. Then graph the function. Show only the portion that makes sense for each situation.

6. On a trip Alex averages 300 mi/day. The distance d he covers is a function of the number of days n.

n				
d				

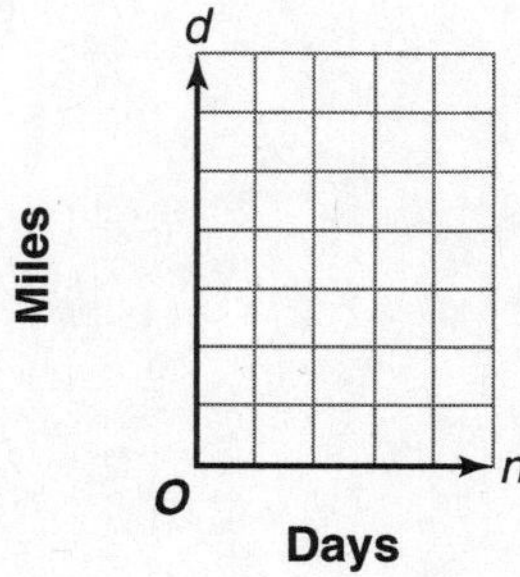

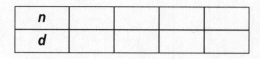

7. Suppose you earn $7 per hour. The number of hours you work n determines your pay p.

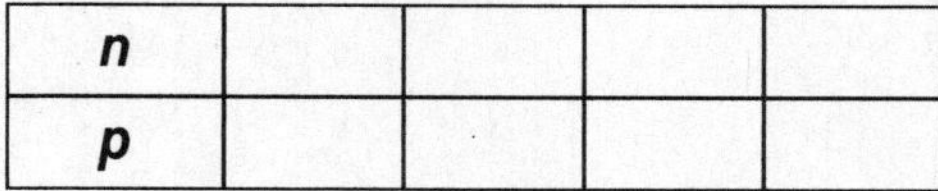

n				
p				

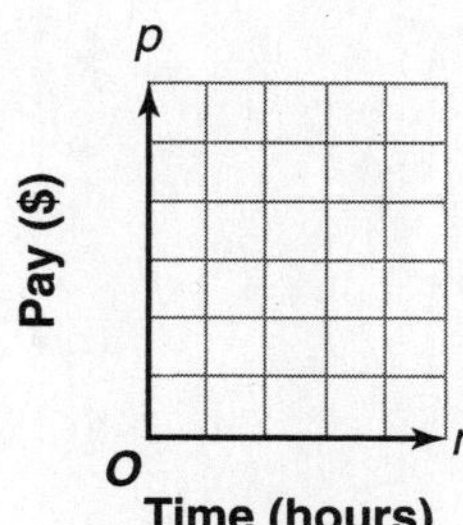

8. Suppose you have $50. The amount of money you spend s decreases the amount you have left a.

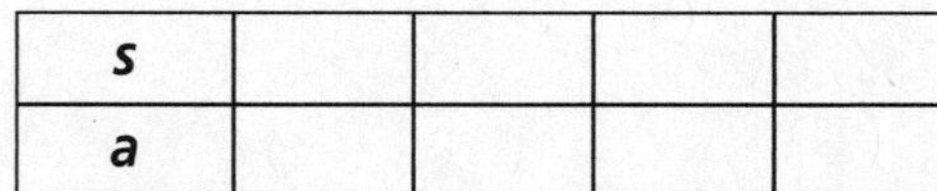

s				
a				

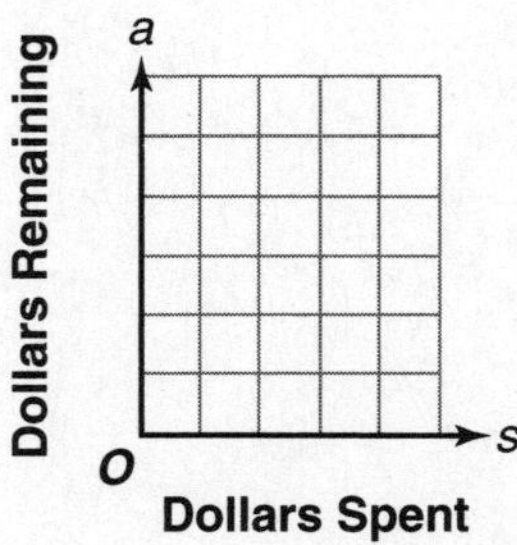

9. You have $10.00. Each week you save $2.50. The number of weeks you save w increases your savings s.

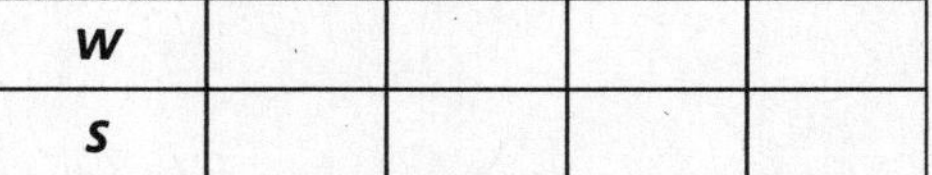

w				
s				

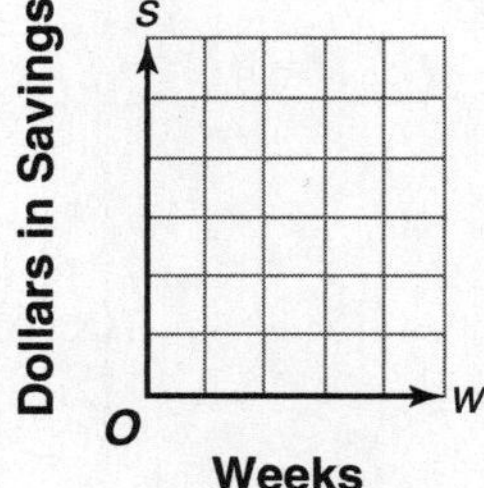

Skill: Solving Equations

Solve each equation.

1. $4r + 6 = 14$

2. $9y - 11 = 7$

3. $\frac{m}{4} + 6 = 3$

4. $-5b - 6 = -11$

5. $\frac{v}{-7} + 8 = 19$

6. $15w - 21 = -111$

7. $7 - 2n = n - 14$

8. $3d + 8 = 2d - 7$

9. $7x - 8 = 3x + 12$

10. $6k - 25 = 7 - 2k$

Skill: Solving Equations *(continued)*

For Exercises 11–14, solve each equation. Check your answer.

11. $3h - 5h + 11 = 17$

12. $7g + 14 - 5g = -8$

13. $4 = 0.4(3d - 5)$

14. $\frac{2}{3}g + \frac{1}{2}g = 14$

15. The perimeter of a pool table is 30 feet. The table is twice as long as it is wide. What is the length ℓ of the pool table? Write an equation to model the situation. Then solve the equation for ℓ.

Name ______________________ Date ____________ Class ____________

Additional Practice

Investigation 2

For Exercises 1–4, write an equation and sketch a graph for the line that meets the given conditions.

1. A line with slope 3.5 and *y*-intercept (0, 4)

2. A line with slope $\frac{3}{2}$ that passes through the point (–2, 0)

3. A line that passes through the points (2, 7) and (6, 15)

4. A line that passes through the points (2, 1) and (6, 9)

For Exercises 5–8, write an equation for the line shown. Identify the slope and *y*-intercept.

5. 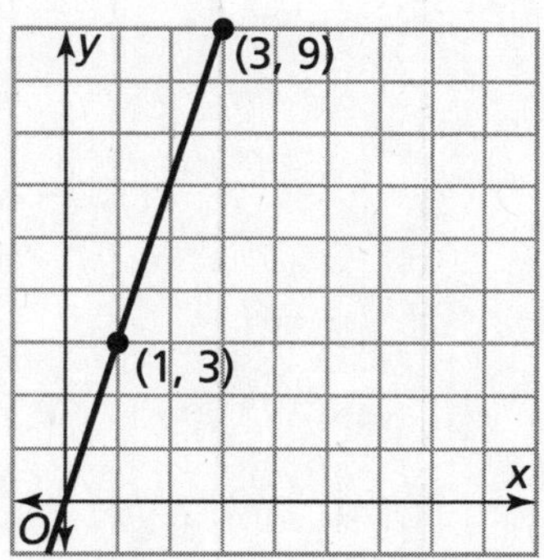

6. 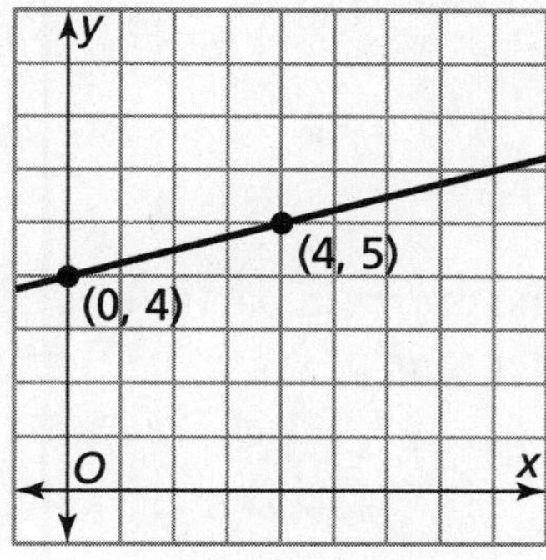

7. 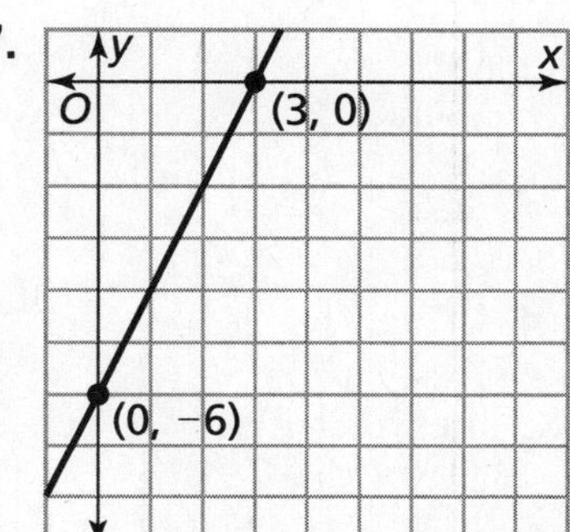

8. 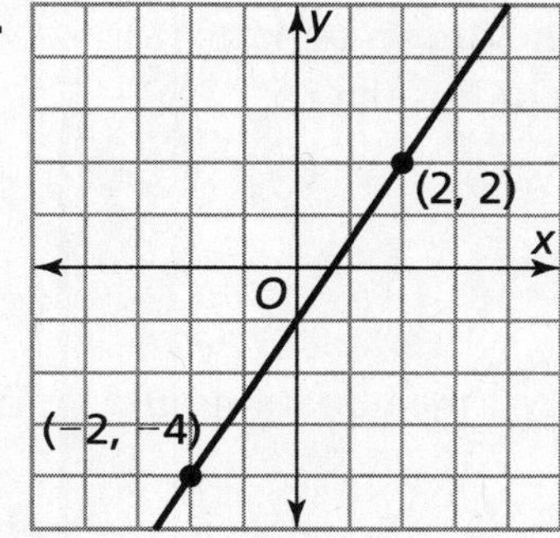

9. For parts (a)–(c), write an equation and sketch a graph for the line that meets the given conditions. Use one set of axes for all three graphs.

   a. A line with slope $\frac{2}{3}$ and y-intercept $(0, 0)$

   b. A line with slope $\frac{2}{3}$ that passes through the point $(6, 6)$

   c. A line with slope $\frac{2}{3}$ that passes through the point $(6, 2)$

   d. What do you notice about the equations and graphs of the three lines?

Additional Practice *(continued)*

10. For parts (a)–(c), write an equation and sketch a graph for a line that meets the given conditions. Use one set of axes for all three graphs.

a. A line with slope 3 and *y*-intercept (0, 5)

b. A line parallel to the line drawn in part (a) with a *y*-intercept greater than 5

c. A line parallel to the line drawn in parts (a) and (b) with a *y*-intercept less than 5

d. What do you notice about the equations and graphs of the three lines?

For Exercises 11–12, write an equation and sketch a graph for the line that meets the given conditions.

11. A line with slope $-\frac{15}{5}$ that passes through the point $(-2.5, 4.5)$

12. A line that passes through the points $(2, -9)$ and $(-2, 3)$

For Exercises 13–14, write an equation for the line shown. Identify the slope and *y*-intercept.

13.

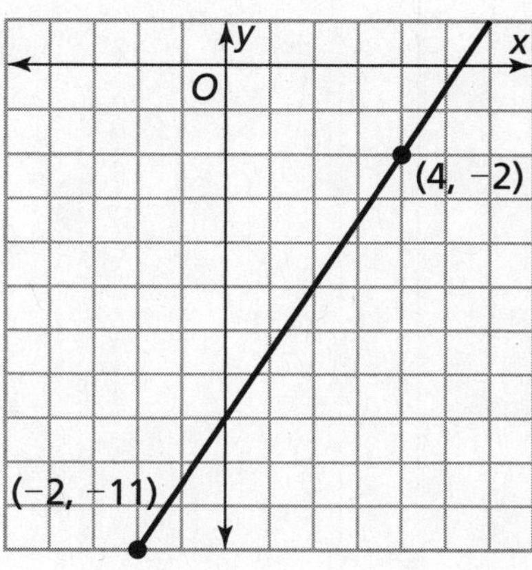

14.

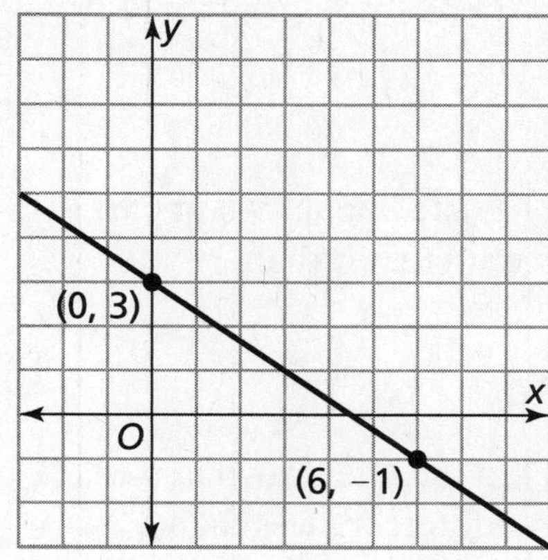

15. For parts (a)–(c), write an equation and sketch a graph for the line that meets the given conditions. Use one set of axes for all three graphs.

a. A line with slope -2 and y-intercept $(0, 0)$

b. A line with slope -2 that passes through the point $(3, -3)$

c. A line with slope -2 that passes through the point $(3, -9)$

d. What do you notice about the equations and graphs of the three lines?

16. For parts (a)–(c), write an equation and sketch a graph for a line that meets the given conditions. Use one set of axes for all three graphs.

a. A line with slope $-\frac{1}{2}$ and y-intercept $(0, 3)$

b. A line parallel to the line drawn in part (a) with a y-intercept greater than 3

c. A line parallel to the line drawn in parts (a) and (b) with a y-intercept less than 3

d. What do you notice about the equations and graphs of the three lines?

17. a. Predict how high a stack of 10 cups would be.

Stack of Styrofoam Cups

Number of Cups	1	2	3	4
Height of the Stack of Cups (cm)	7	8	9	10

b. Describe the pattern in words.

c. Describe the pattern with an equation. Let x represent the number of cups and h the height.

d. What does the coefficient of x mean in this context? Does it have a unit of measure? Explain.

e. What does the constant term mean in this context? Does it have a unit of measure? Explain.

18. To the right are the graphs of three lines.

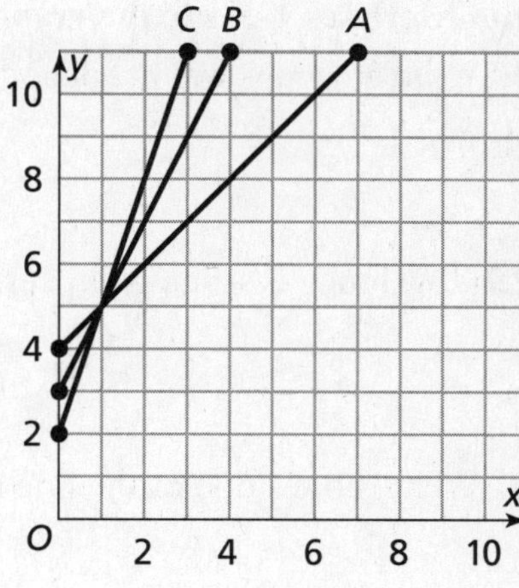

a. Match each line with its rule.

$y = x + 4$ $y = 2x + 3$ $y = 3x + 2$

b. For each equation, what are the y-values when $x = 3$? When $x = 4$?

c. Why are the y-values "farther apart" when $x = 4$ than when $x = 3$?

19. Find exact solutions for each of these equations.

a. $9 - x = 3x - 7$ **b.** $3.6x + 2.4 = 2.1x - 0.6$

20. Find at least three values of x for which the inequality is true.

a. $5x - 3 \leq 12$ **b.** $8x - 1 \leq 4x + 7$

Skill: Using Linear Models

For Exercises 1–5, use the graph at the right.

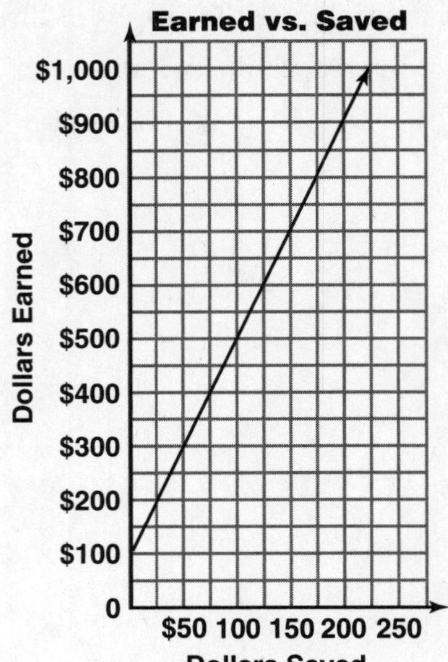

1. What earnings will produce $225 in savings?

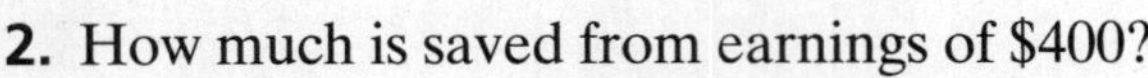

2. How much is saved from earnings of $400?

3. What is the slope of the line in the graph?

4. For each increase of $200 in earnings, what is the increase in savings?

5. Write an equation for the line.

6. A ride in a cab costs $0.40 plus $0.15 per mile.

   a. Write and graph an equation for traveling x miles in the cab.

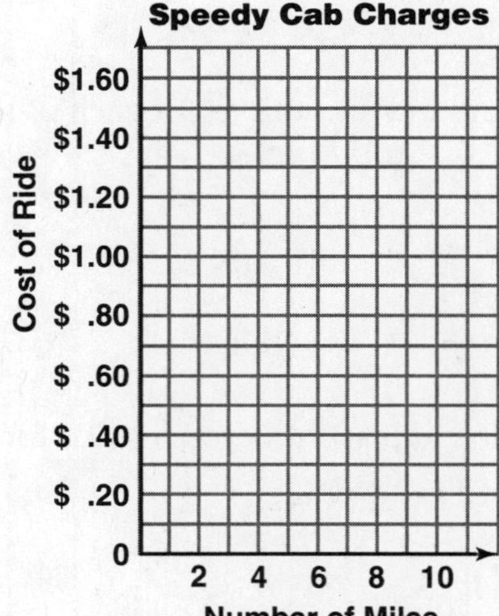

   b. The cab charges $0.70 for a ride of how many miles?

   c. How much does the cab charge for a trip of 8 miles?

Name ______________________________ Date __________ Class __________

Skill: Using Linear Models *(continued)*

Investigation 2

Thinking With Mathematical Models

A giraffe was 1 foot tall at birth, 7 feet tall at the age of 4, and $11\frac{1}{2}$ feet tall at the age of 7.

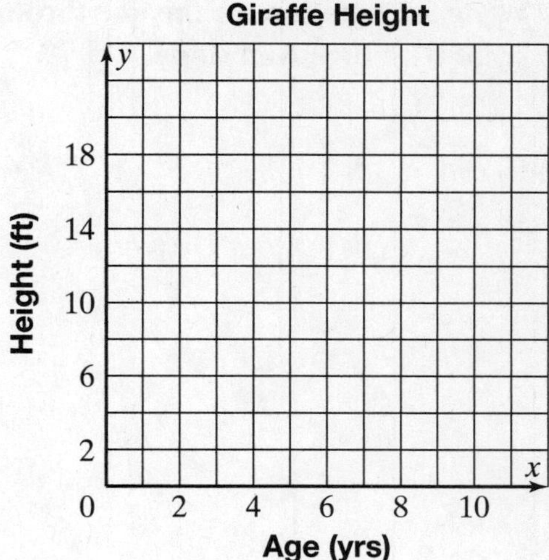

7. Plot the data.

8. Draw a line that models the pattern in the data.

9. Write an equation for your line.

10. Use your equation to find the following information.

a. the giraffe's height at the age of 5

b. the age at which the giraffe was 16 ft tall

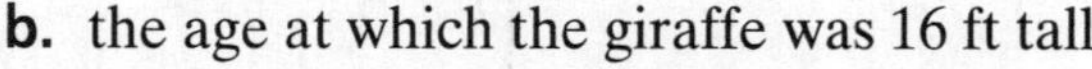

A hippopotamus weighed 700 pounds at the age of 1, 1,900 pounds at the age of 3, and 2,500 pounds at the age of 4.

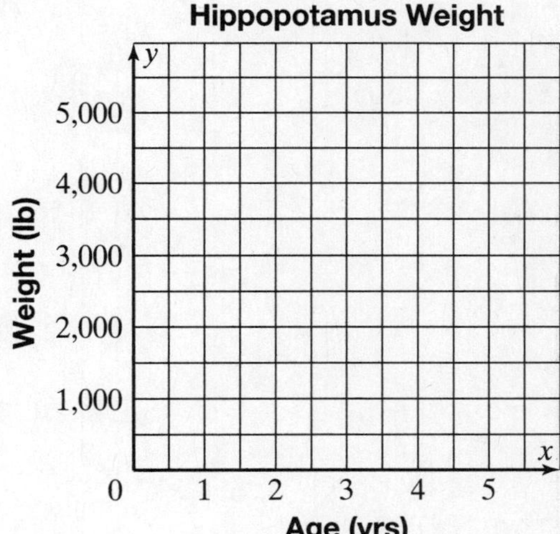

11. Plot the data.

12. Draw a line that models the pattern in the data.

13. Write an equation for your line.

14. Use the equation to predict the following information.

a. the hippo's weight at the age of 8

b. the age at which the hippo weighed 7,900 pounds

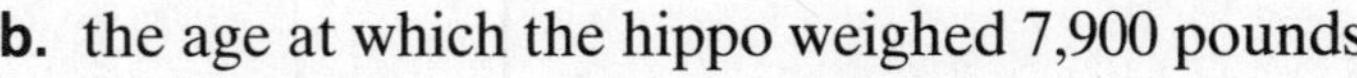

Name ______________________________ Date ____________ Class ____________

Skill: Writing Equations of Lines

Write an equation for the line through the given points or through the given point with the given slope.

1. $(5, 7), (6, 8)$

2. $(-2, 3)$; slope $= -1$

3. $(1, 2), (3, 8)$

4. $(-2, 3)$; slope $= 4$

5. $(4, 7)$; slope $= \frac{3}{2}$

6. $(6, -2)$; slope $= -\frac{4}{3}$

7. $(0, 5), (-3, 2)$

8. $(8, 11), (6, 16)$

Name ______________________________ Date __________ Class __________

Skill: Writing Equations of Lines *(continued)*

Investigation 2

Thinking With Mathematical Models

Is the relationship shown by the data linear? If it is, model the data with an equation.

9.

x	y
2	3
3	7
4	11
5	15

10.

x	y
−3	4
−1	6
1	7
3	10

11.

x	y
−2	5
3	−5
7	−13
11	−21

Write an equation of each line.

12.

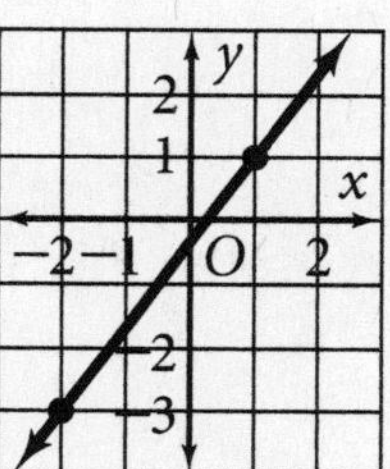

13.

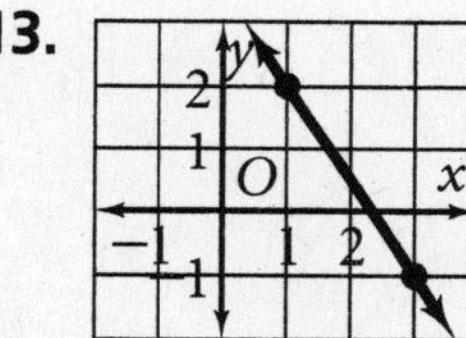

14.

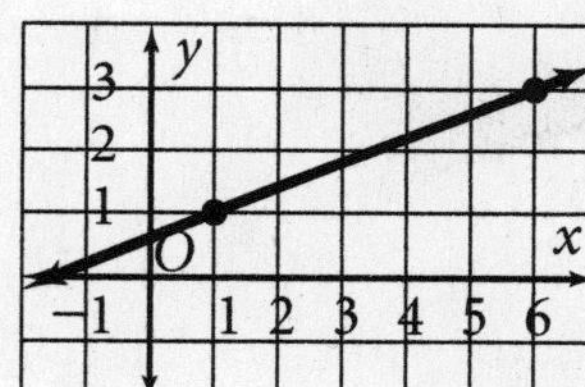

Name ______________________________ Date ____________ Class ____________

Skill: Solving Inequalities

Investigation 2

Thinking With Mathematical Models

Determine whether each number is a solution of the given inequality.

1. $x \leq -8$ **a.** -10 **b.** 6 **c.** -8

2. $-1 > x$ **a.** 0 **b.** -3 **c.** -6

3. $w < \frac{18}{7}$ **a.** 5 **b.** -2 **c.** $3\frac{1}{2}$

4. $0.65 \geq y$ **a.** 0.43 **b.** -0.65 **c.** 0.56

5. $2y + 1 > -5$ **a.** -4 **b.** -2 **c.** 4

6. $7x - 14 \leq 6x - 16$ **a.** 0 **b.** -4 **c.** 2

7. $n(n - 6) \geq -4$ **a.** 3 **b.** -2 **c.** 5

Write an inequality for each situation.

8. Everyone in the class is under 13 years old. Let x be the age of a person in the class.

9. The speed limit is 60 miles per hour. Let s be the speed of a car driving within the limit.

10. You have \$4.50 to spend on lunch. Let c be the cost of your lunch.

Name ______________________________ Date ____________ Class ____________

Additional Practice

1. Suppose you are designing a rectangular garden with an area of 350 square feet.
   - **a.** What perimeters can you make the garden using whole numbers? For each perimeter, give the length and the width.
   - **b.** Suppose you know the length L of a rectangle with an area of 350 square feet. Write an equation that would help you to determine the width W.
   - **c.** Suppose you know the width W of a rectangle with an area of 350 square feet. Write an equation that would help you to determine the length L.
   - **d.** Make a graph using the equation you wrote in part (b). Explain what your graph is showing.

2. Use only the first quadrant of the coordinate grid for this problem. If you are using a graphing calculator, set your window to show x and y values from 0 to 10 with a scale of 1. Show each graph on the same set of axes.
   - **a.** Graph the equation $y = \frac{10}{x}$ for x values from 1 to 10. For which value of x (from 1 to 10) is y the greatest? For which value of x is y the least?
   - **b.** Graph the equation $y = 10x$ for x values from 1 to 10. For which value of x (from 1 to 10) is y the greatest? For which value of x is y the least?
   - **c.** Compare the greatest and least values for y that you found in parts (a) and (b).
   - **d.** At what point do the two graphs intersect?

Name ______________________________ Date ____________ Class ____________

Additional Practice (continued)

Investigation 3

3. Carl wants to save $1,000 for a trip.

a. Suppose he saves $10 per week. How many weeks will it take? How many weeks at $20 per week? How many weeks at $30 per week?

b. Complete this table and then draw a graph to show the data.

Carl's Savings

Amount Saved per Week	10	20	30	40	50	60	70
Number of Weeks							

c. Write an equation showing the relationship between the amount a saved per week and the number of weeks n.

d. What are the changes in the number of weeks needed to reach $1,000 when the amount saved per week changes from:

i. $10 to $20

ii. $20 to $30

iii. $30 to $40

e. How do the answers to part (d) show that the relationship between *amount saved per week* and *number of weeks* is not linear?

4. Tamika is organizing a walkathon for her class. The goal is for students to walk a total of 500 miles. Each student who participates will walk 1 mile per day.

a. How many days will it take to reach the goal if Tamika is the only student who participates?

Additional Practice *(continued)*

b. How many days will it take to reach the goal if 5 students participate? How many days if 10 students participate? How many days if 25 students participate?

c. Make a table of data.

500-Mile Walkathon

Number of Students	1	2	3	4	5	6	7	8	9	10	11	12	13
Number of Days													

Number of Students	14	15	16	17	18	19	20	21	22	23	24	25
Number of Days												

d. Make a graph of the data.

e. Should the points be connected? Explain your reasoning.

f. What pattern do you notice for the number of days when there are 1, 2, 4, 8, and 16 students participating?

g. How do the data in the table show that the relationship between *number of students participating* and *number of day* is not linear?

h. Write an equation showing the relationship between the number of students s participating and the number of days n required to reach the goal.

Additional Practice *(continued)*

5. How are the length and width of rectangles related if the area is fixed at 60 cm^2?

a. Make a table of lengths and widths. Draw a graph of these data.

b. Should the points be connected? Explain your reasoning.

c. Write an equation showing the relationship between length ℓ and width w.

d. Is the relationship between *length* and *width* linear when the area is constant? How does the graph show this?

6. How are the length and width of rectangles related if the perimeter is fixed at 60 cm?

a. Make a table of lengths and widths. Draw a graph of these data.

b. Should the points be connected? Why?

c. Write an equation showing the relationship between length ℓ and width w.

d. Is the relationship between *length* and *width* linear when the perimeter is constant? How does the graph show this?

Name ______________________________ Date __________ Class __________

Skill: Identifying Inverse Variation

Investigation 3

Thinking With Mathematical Models

Tell whether the relationship between *x* and *y* is an *inverse variation.* If it is, write an equation for the relationship.

1.

x	1	7	14
y	70	10	5

2.

x	2	3	4
y	24	16	12

3.

x	5	6	7
y	55	66	77

4.

x	2	4	8
y	9	18	36

5.

x	2	3	4
y	18	12	9

6.

x	1	2	3
y	6	3	2

Name ______________________ Date ___________ Class ___________

Additional Practice

Investigation 1

Looking for Pythagoras

For Exercises 1–3, refer to the map on the following page.

1. Which landmarks are 5 blocks apart by car?

2. The taxi stand is 5 blocks by car from the hospital and 5 blocks by car from the police station. Give the coordinates of the taxi stand.

3. The airport is halfway between City Hall and the hospital by helicopter. Give the coordinates of the airport.

4. Let a right triangle with vertices at $(0, 0)$, $(1, 0)$ and $(0, 1)$ be the unit for measuring area in the following questions.

   a. Draw a square with vertices $(0, 1)$, $(1, 0)$, $(0, -1)$, and $(-1, 0)$. What is the area of this square in the triangle units described above?

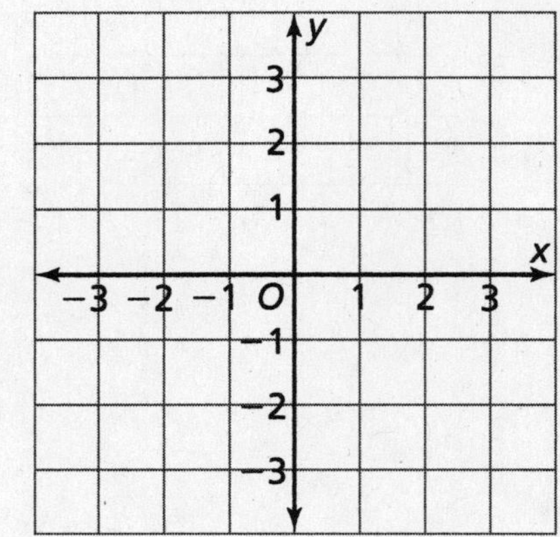

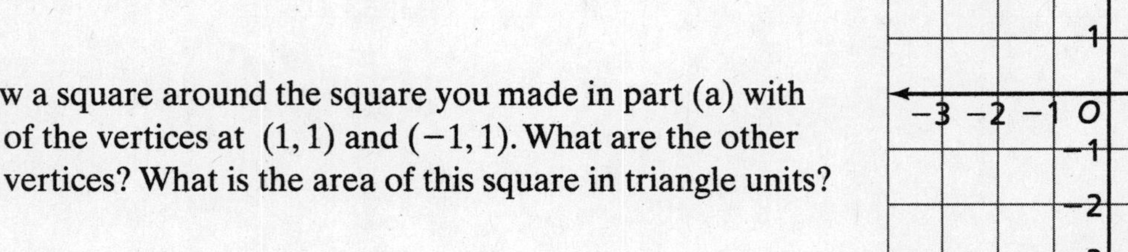

   b. Draw a square around the square you made in part (a) with two of the vertices at $(1, 1)$ and $(-1, 1)$. What are the other two vertices? What is the area of this square in triangle units?

   c. Draw the square of the next size. One of its vertices is $(0, -2)$. What are the other three vertices? What is the area of this square in triangle units?

   d. What are the four vertices of the square of the next size? What is its area in triangle units?

   e. What do you notice about the areas of the squares, as the squares get larger?

Name ________________________________ Date ___________ Class ___________

Additional Practice *(continued)*

For Exercises 5–10, use the given lengths to find the area of each figure. Show your calculations. Record which formulas you can use as part of your reasoning.

5.

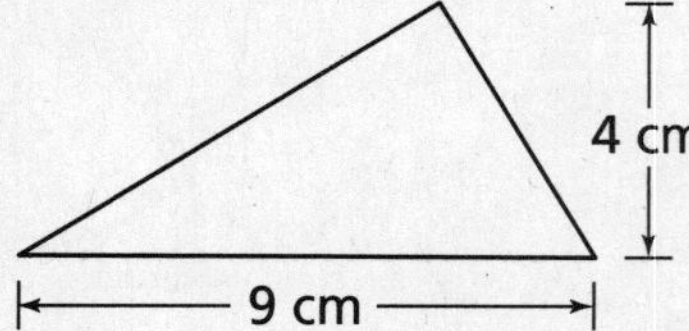

6.

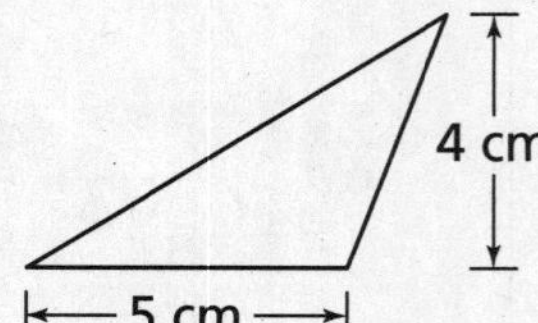

7.

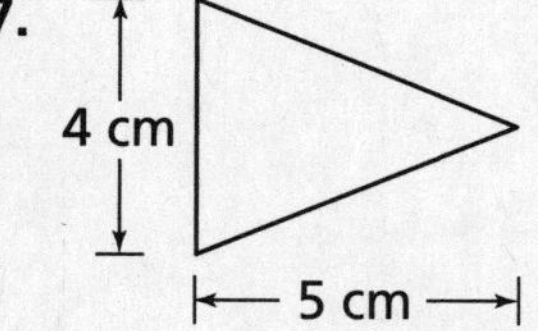

8.

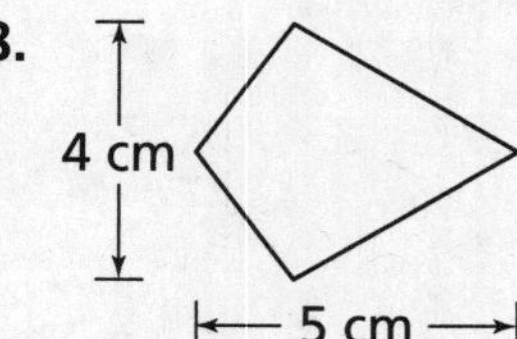

9.

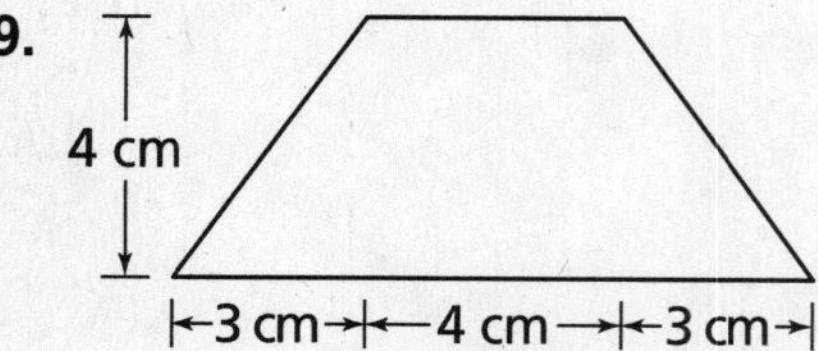

10.

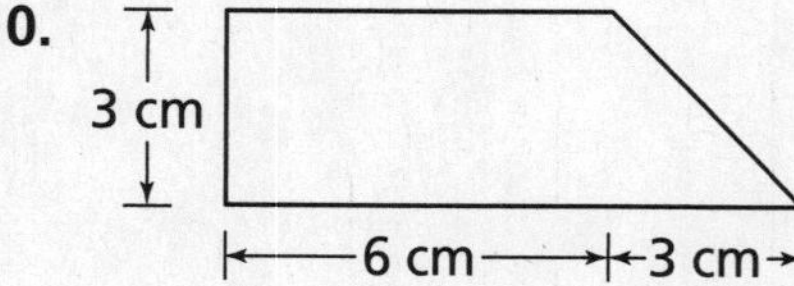

Additional Practice *(continued)*

For Exercises 11–14, find the area of the figure. Explain our reasoning.

11.

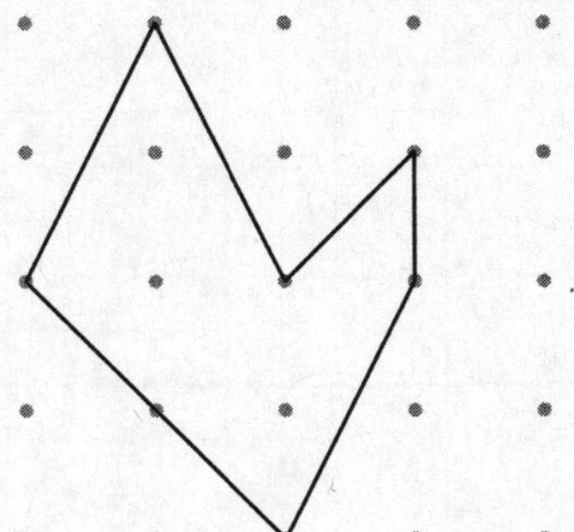

12.

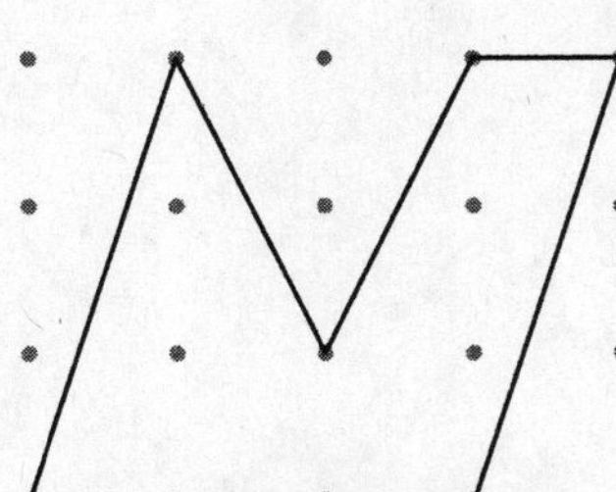

13.

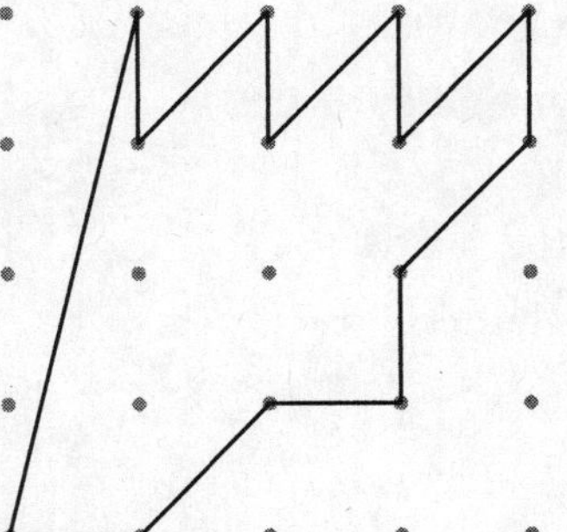

14.

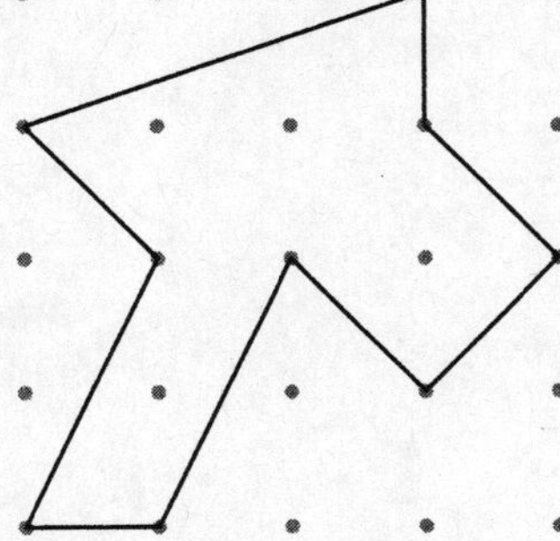

Name ______________________ Date ____________ Class ____________

Skill: Graphing Equations

Investigation 1

Looking for Pythagoras

Name the coordinates of each point in the graph.

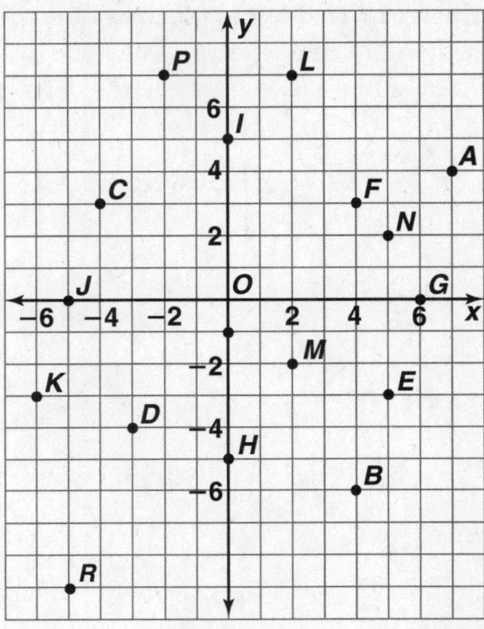

1. *J*
2. *R*
3. *K*
4. *M*
5. *I*
6. *P*
7. *N*
8. *L*

9. Arnie plotted points on the graph below. He placed his pencil point at *A*. He can move either right or down any number of units until he reaches point *B*. In how many ways can he do this?

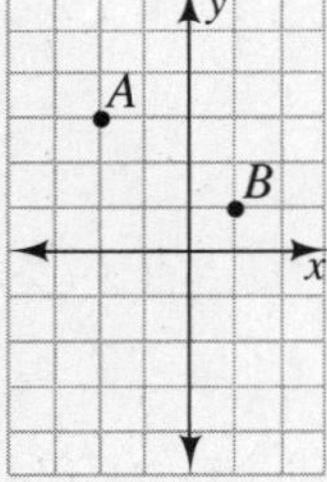

10. Marika had to draw $\triangle ABC$ that fit several requirements.
   a. It must fit in the box shown.
   b. The side $\overline{AB}$ has coordinates $A(-2, 0)$ and $B(2, 0)$.
   c. Point *C* must be on the *y*-axis.

   Name all the points that could be point *C*.

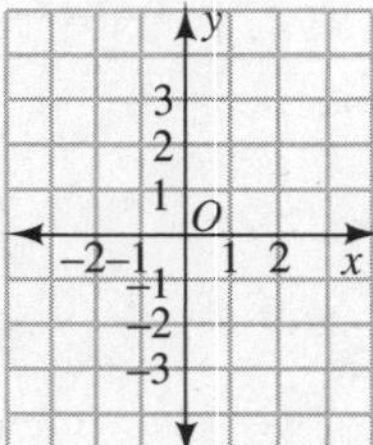

Name ______________________ Date __________ Class __________

Additional Practice

In Problem 2.3, you found the lengths of line segments drawn on 5-dot-by-5-dot grids. Some of those lengths were written as square roots, such as $\sqrt{2}$. When you enter $\sqrt{2}$ in your calculator, the result is a decimal with a value of approximately 1.4.

For Exercises 1–6, find the approximate value for the given length to the nearest tenth.

1. $\sqrt{5}$

2. $\sqrt{13}$

3. $\sqrt{20}$

4. $\sqrt{17}$

5. $\sqrt{2} + \sqrt{5}$

6. $\sqrt{8} + 6 + \sqrt{10}$

7. Is $\sqrt{8} + \sqrt{10}$ the same as $\sqrt{8 + 10}$? Explain your answer in two ways:

a. Use your calculator to help give a numerical argument.

b. Use a grid and lengths of line segments to give a geometric argument.

Name ______________________ Date ____________ Class ____________

Additional Practice *(continued)*

For Exercises 8–10, find the perimeter of each figure. Express the perimeter in two ways: as the sum of a whole number and square roots, and as a single value after using decimal approximations to the nearest tenth for the square roots. An example is done for you.

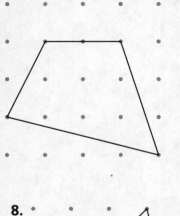

The perimeter of this figure is
$2 + \sqrt{10} + \sqrt{17} + \sqrt{5} \approx$
$2 + 3.2 + 4.1 + 2.2 =$
11.5 units

8.

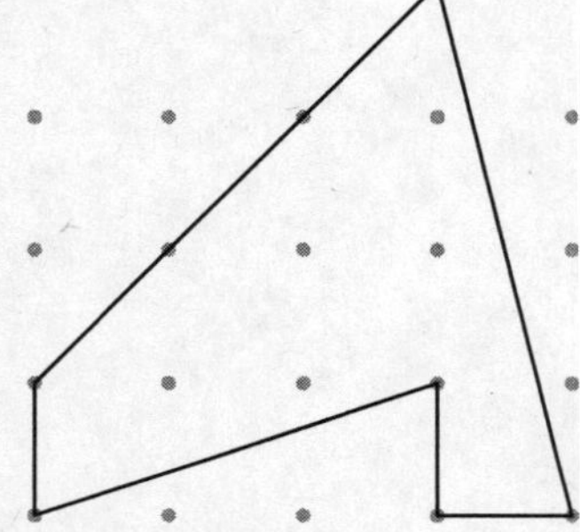

9.

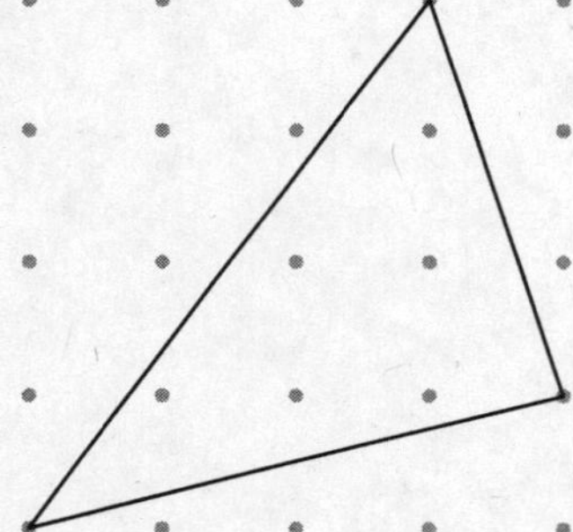

10.

Name ______________________ Date ____________ Class ____________

Additional Practice *(continued)*

11. For each number sentence below, decide if it is true (T) or false (F):

a. $7 = \sqrt{49}$

b. $7 = -\sqrt{49}$

c. $-7 = \sqrt{49}$

d. $-7 = -\sqrt{49}$

12. Points A, B, C, D, and E are shown on the grid below:

• A	•	•	•	•
•	• B	•	•	•
•	•	• C	•	•
•	•	•	• D	•
•	•	•	•	• E

Using these 5 points only, list all line segments which have the following lengths:

$\sqrt{2}$

$2\sqrt{2}$

$3\sqrt{2}$

$4\sqrt{2}$

$5\sqrt{2}$

13. List all the whole numbers that could be substituted for x so that the expression is true.

a. $4 < \sqrt{x} < 5$

b. $8 < \sqrt{x} < 9$

c. $0 < \sqrt{x} < 1$

Name ______________________________ Date __________ Class __________

Skill: Exponents and Square Roots

Investigation 2

Looking for Pythagoras

Find the value of each square root.

1. $\sqrt{64}$ **2.** $\sqrt{81}$ **3.** $\sqrt{100}$ **4.** $\sqrt{144}$

Find the length of the side of a square with the given area.

5. 121 ft^2 **6.** 4 mi^2

7. 225 $in.^2$ **8.** 196 yd^2

Find two consecutive whole numbers that each number is between.

9. $\sqrt{80}$ **10.** $\sqrt{56}$

11. $\sqrt{130}$ **12.** $\sqrt{150}$

13. $\sqrt{70}$ **14.** $\sqrt{190}$

15. $\sqrt{204}$ **16.** $\sqrt{159}$

Estimate each square root to one decimal place.

17. $\sqrt{18}$ **18.** $\sqrt{24}$

19. $\sqrt{50}$ **20.** $\sqrt{8}$

Name ______________________ Date ____________ Class ____________

Additional Practice

Investigation 3

Looking for Pythagoras

1. a. Find the length of the hypotenuse of each triangle.

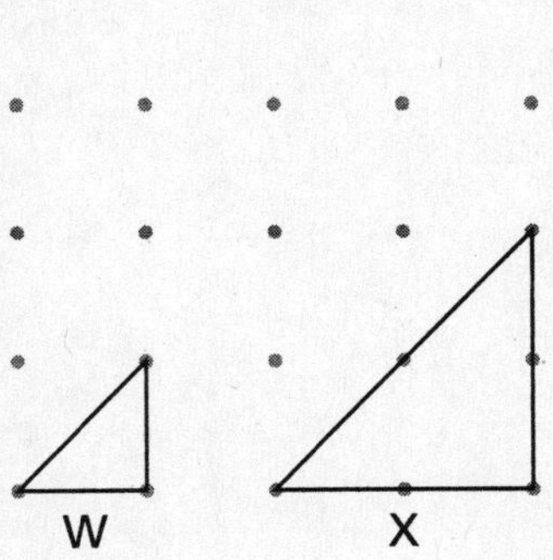

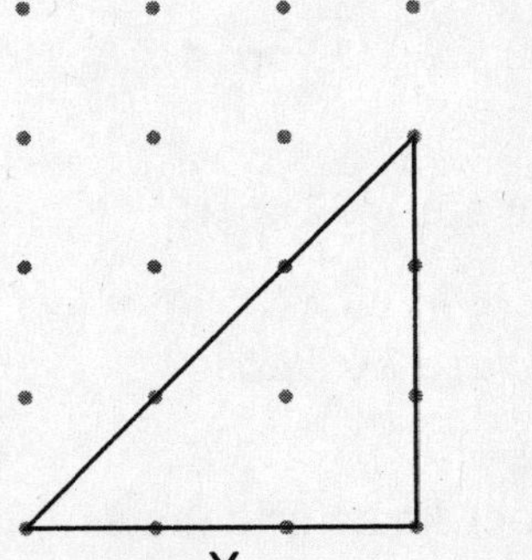

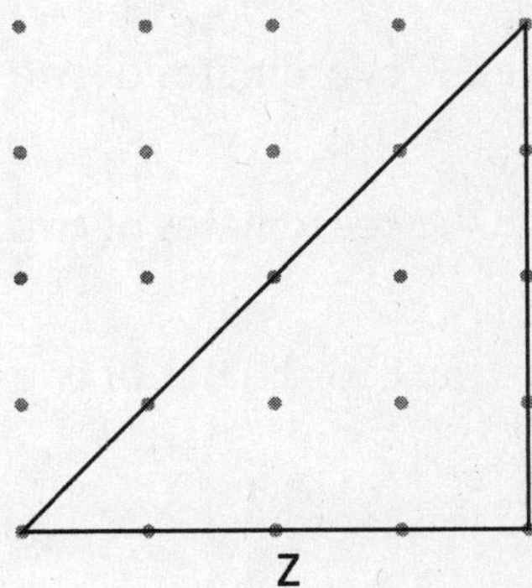

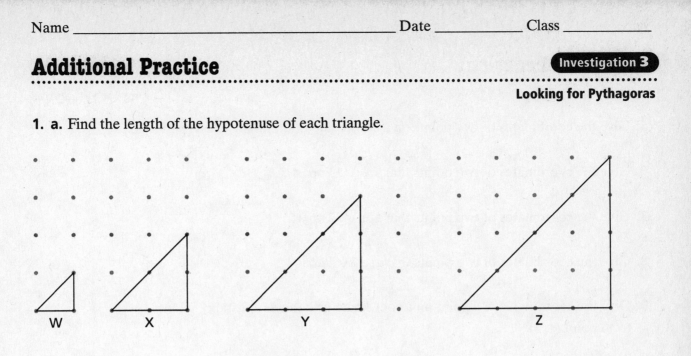

b. How are the hypotenuse lengths in figures X, Y, and Z related to the hypotenuse length in figure W?

2. Draw a right triangle with a hypotenuse length of $\sqrt{5}$.

3. Draw a right triangle with a hypotenuse length of $2\sqrt{5}$.

4. Draw a right triangle with a hypotenuse length of $3\sqrt{5}$.

Additional Practice *(continued)*

5. Give the coordinates of two points on a coordinate grid that are $\sqrt{10}$ apart.

6. Give the coordinates of two points that are $\sqrt{13}$ apart.

7. Give the coordinates of two points that are $\sqrt{32}$ apart.

8. Give the coordinates of two points that are $7\sqrt{2}$ apart.

9. Give the coordinates of a point on a coordinate grid that is a distance of $\sqrt{5}$ from point $(1, 3)$.

10. Give the coordinates of a point that is a distance of $\sqrt{17}$ from point $(0, -5)$.

11. Give the coordinates of a point that is a distance of $2\sqrt{5}$ from point $(-10, -2)$.

12. Give the coordinates of a point that is a distance of $3\sqrt{5}$ from point $(8, -2)$.

13. What is the length of the line segment that connects points $(0, 0)$ and $(4, 2)$?

14. What is the length of the line segment that connects points $(0, 0)$ and $(2, 4)$?

15. What is the length of the line segment that connects points $(-2, 0)$ and $(0, 2)$?

16. What is the length of the line segment that connects points $(0, -3)$ and $(3, 3)$?

Name ______________________________ Date ____________ Class ____________

Additional Practice *(continued)*

For Exercises 17–19, find the perimeter of the figure to the nearest tenth of a centimeter.

17.

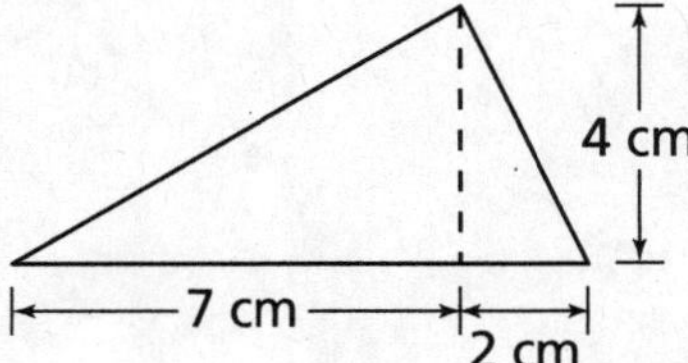

18.

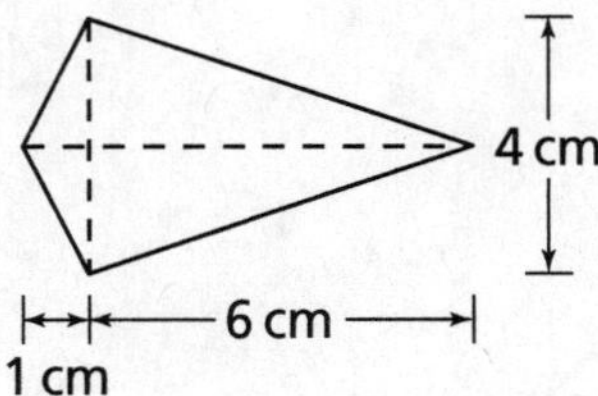

19.

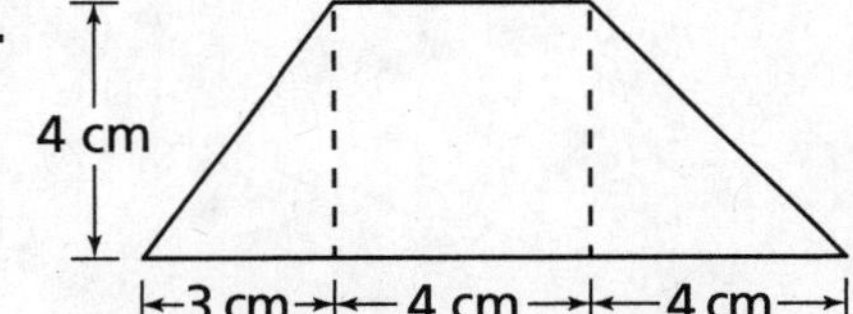

For Exercises 20–23, use the map in Additional Practice, Investigation 1 to find the distance by helicopter between the two landmarks. Explain how you found the distance.

20. the greenhouse and the police station

21. the police station and the art museum

22. the greenhouse and City Hall

23. City Hall and the animal shelter

Name ______________________ Date ____________ Class ____________

Additional Practice *(continued)*

For Exercises 24–26, find the perimeter of the right triangle. Express the perimeter as the sum of a whole number and square roots and as a single value using decimal approximations to the nearest tenth for the square roots. An example is done for you.

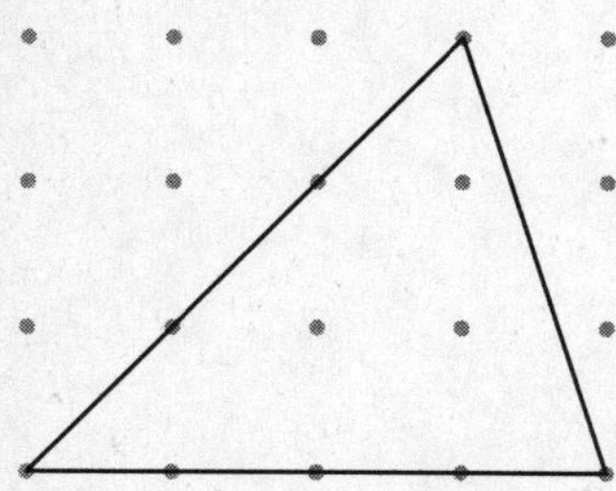

The perimeter of this figure is
$4 + \sqrt{10} + \sqrt{18} \approx 2 + 3.2 + 4. = 9.4$ units

24.

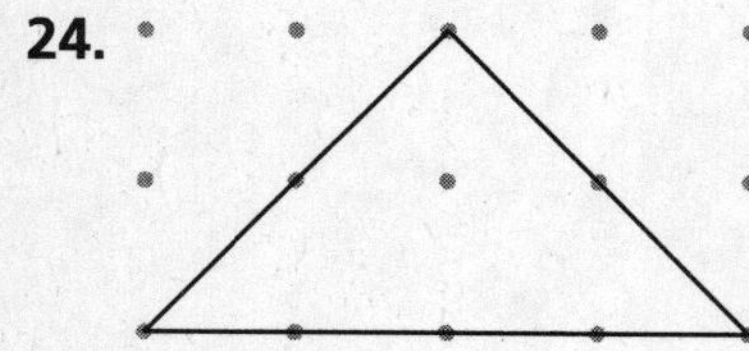

25.

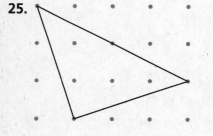

26.

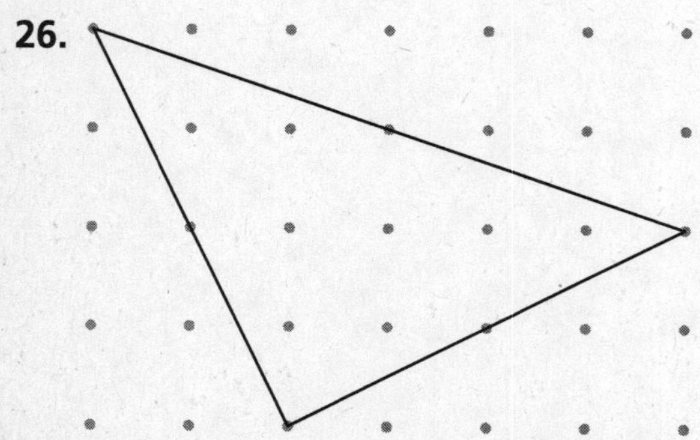

Name ______________________ Date ____________ Class ____________

Skill: Using the Pythagorean Theorem

Can you form a right triangle with the three lengths given? Show your work.

1. 20, 21, 29

2. 7, 11, 12

3. $10, 2\sqrt{11}, 12$

4. 28, 45, 53

5. $9, \sqrt{10}, 10$

6. 10, 15, 20

Name ______________________ Date ___________ Class ___________

Skill: Using the Pythagorean Theorem *(continued)*

Use the Pythagorean theorem to find the missing side of each right triangle.

7.

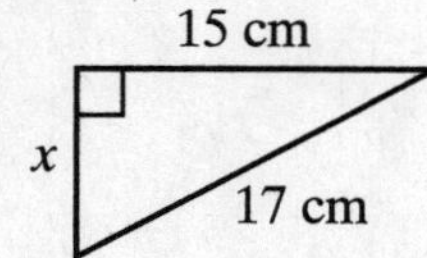

8.

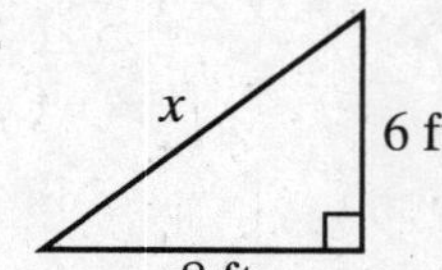

9.

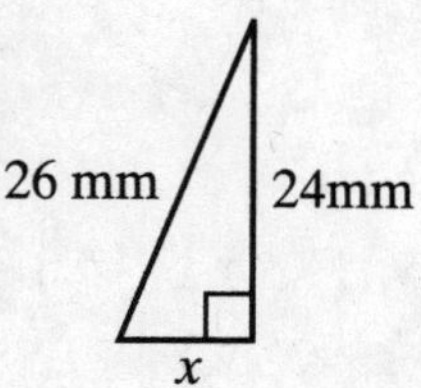

10.

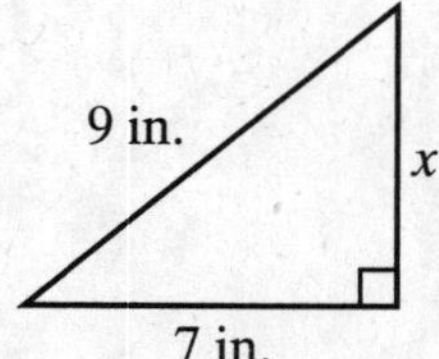

11.

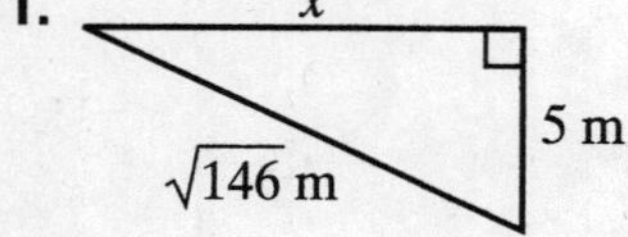

12.

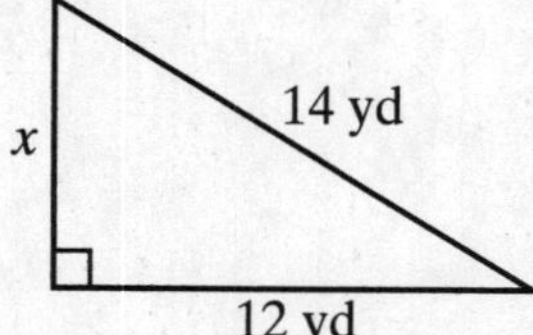

Name ____________________ Date ____________ Class ____________

Additional Practice

Investigation 4

Looking for Pythagoras

Find the length of *AB* to the nearest hundredth centimeter. All measurements are in centimeters, but figures may be drawn to different scales. Explain your reasoning.

1.

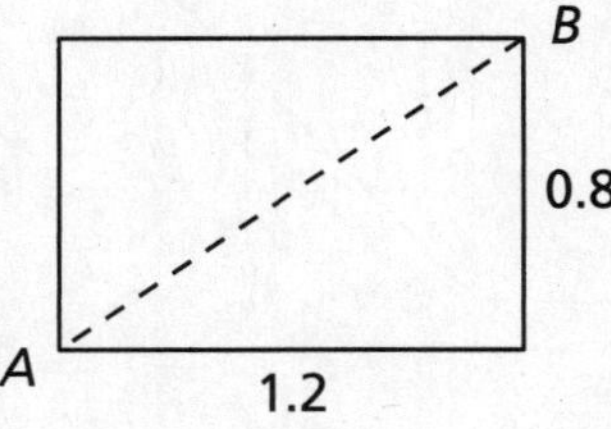

2. This is a regular pentagon.

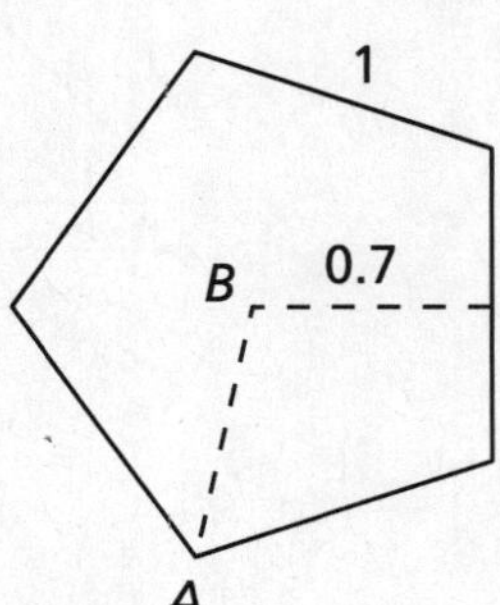

3.

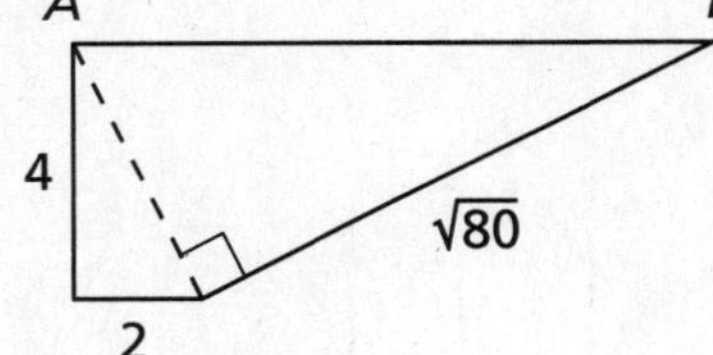

4. This is a regular hexagon.

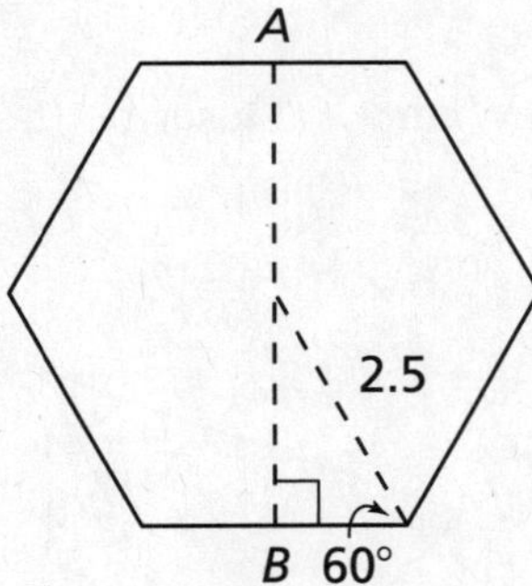

Name ______________________ Date ____________ Class ____________

For Exercises 5–8, find the perimeter of the figure to the nearest tenth centimeter. All measurements are in centimeters, but figures may not be to scale.

5.

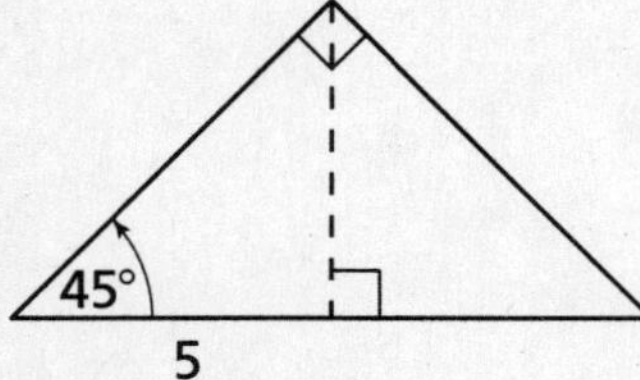

6.

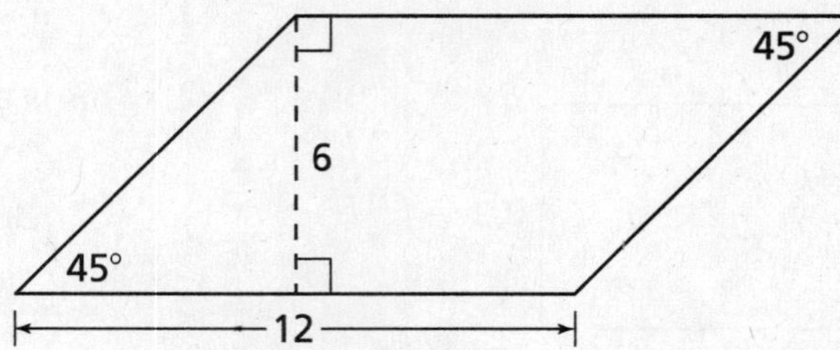

7.

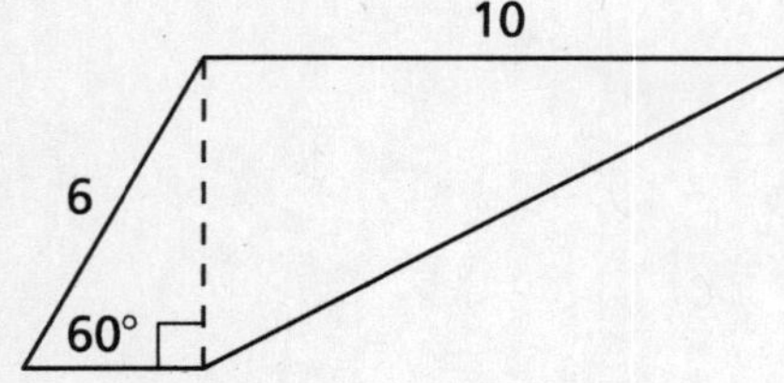

8.

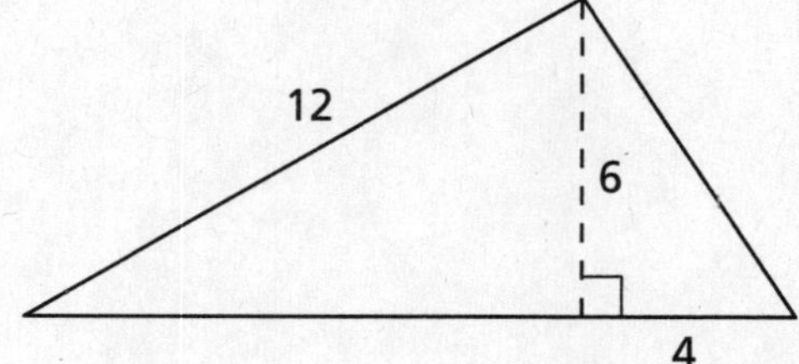

9. a. Find the areas of figures W and X. Describe the method you use.

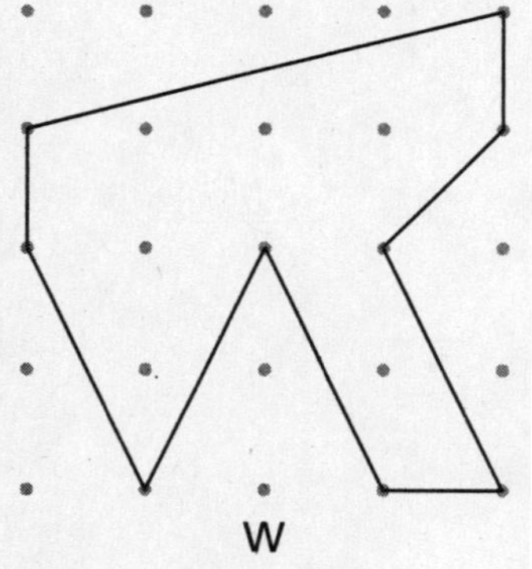

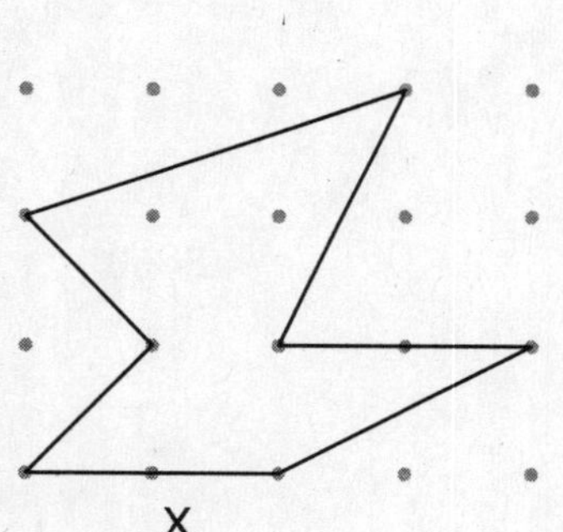

Z

b. On the above grid, draw two different figures Y and Z, each with an area of $7\frac{1}{2}$ square units.

Sketch the triangle described, and label the three side lengths.

10. Two of the sides in this isosceles right triangle measure $\sqrt{18}$ and 3.

11. Two of the sides in this isosceles right triangle measure $\sqrt{52}$ and $\sqrt{26}$.

For Exercises 12–17, a pair of lengths is given. What third length could be used with the other two lengths to make a right triangle?

Try to solve each problem two ways:

(1) let the missing value be the length of one of the legs of the triangle and

(2) let the missing value be the length of the hypotenuse of the triangle. Sketch each triangle you find, and label the side lengths.

12. 9, 15, and □

13. $\sqrt{45}$, 3, and □

14. $\sqrt{50}$, 5, and □

15. $\sqrt{18}$, 3, and □

16. 8, $\sqrt{18}$, and □

17. $\sqrt{52}$, $\sqrt{26}$, and □

Name ______________________________ Date __________ Class __________

Skill: Special Right Triangles

The length of one side of the triangle is given in each row of the table. Find the missing lengths for that triangle.

	m	*n*	*p*
1.	14		
2.			36
3.		$9\sqrt{3}$	
4.	5		

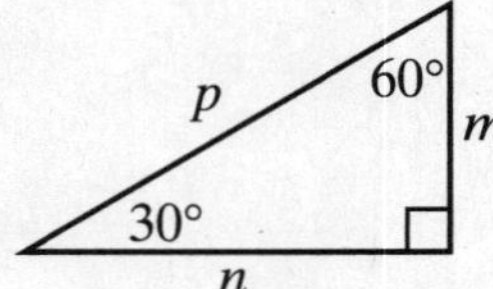

	x	*y*	*z*
5.	11		
6.		8.7	
7.			$7\sqrt{2}$
8.	17		

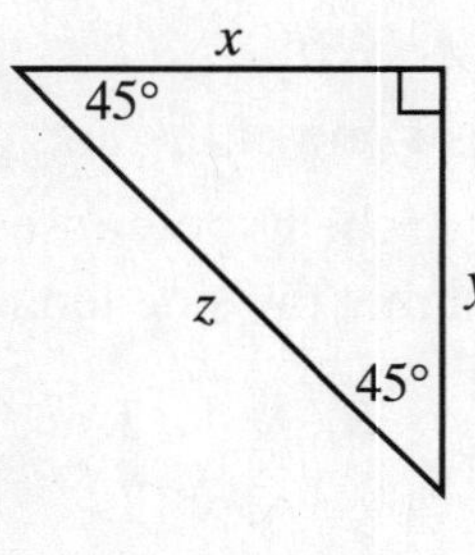

In the figure, $BD = 6\sqrt{2}$. Find each value.

9. AB

10. AD

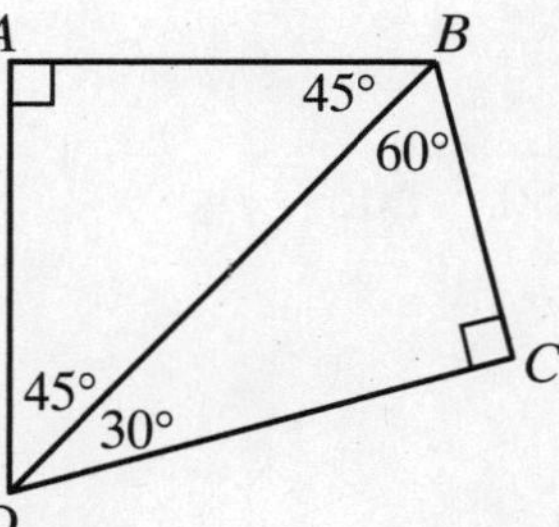

11. BC

12. CD

Name ______________________ Date __________ Class __________

Additional Practice

1. Cut a sheet of paper into fourths. Stack the four pieces and cut the stack into fourths. Stack all the pieces and cut that stack into fourths again.

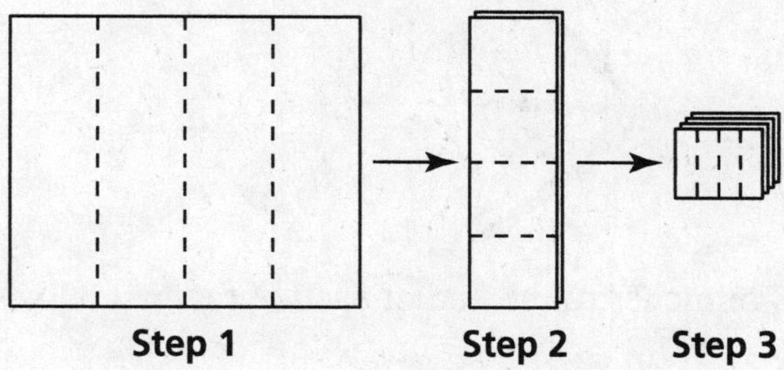

How many pieces of paper would you have at the end of

a. Step 1? **b.** Step 2? **c.** Step 3?

d. Step 10? **e.** Step *n*?

For Exercises 2–5, write the expression in standard form.

2. $2^1 \times 5^1$

3. $2^2 \times 5^2$

4. $2^3 \times 5^3$

5. $2^4 \times 5^4$

Additional Practice *(continued)*

6. Suppose you drew a pattern of branching lines starting with 3 lines:

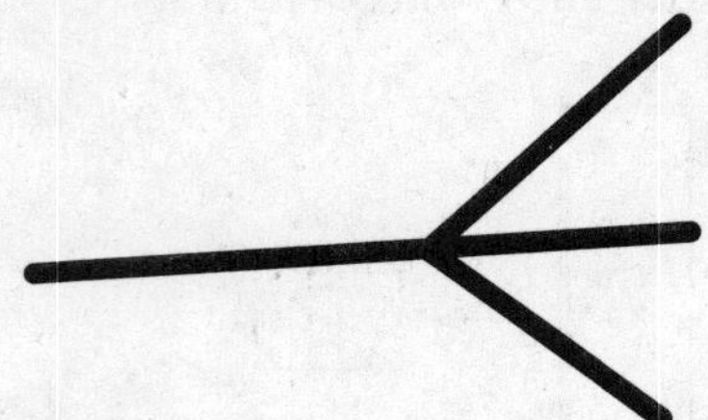

Using a second color, you added 3 branches to the end of each of the first 3 lines:

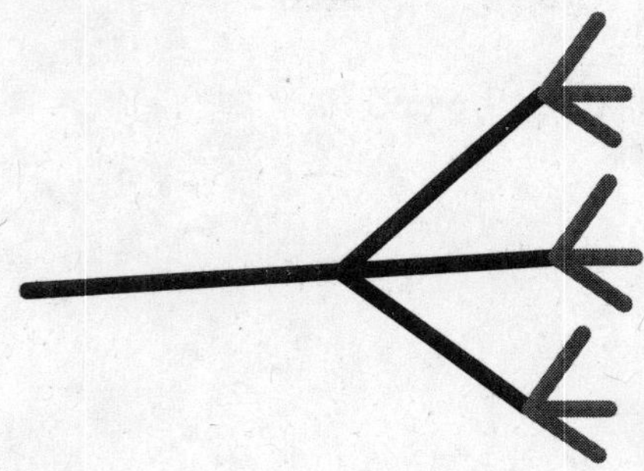

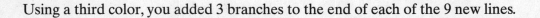

Using a third color, you added 3 branches to the end of each of the 9 new lines.

a. Complete the table to show the number of branches you would draw in each new color.

Color	Branches
1	3
2	9
3	
4	
5	
6	

b. Write an equation showing the relationship between the number of branches drawn *b* and the number of the color *c*.

c. What is the number of the first color with which you will draw at least 1,000 branches?

d. Make a graph of the (color, branches) data from part (a).

Name ______________________________ Date ____________ Class ____________

Skill: Using Exponents

Investigation 1

Growing, Growing, Growing

Write each expression in exponential form.

1. $3 \times 3 \times 3 \times 3 \times 3$

2. $2.7 \times 2.7 \times 2.7$

3. $2 \times 2 \times 2 \times 2 \times 2 \times 2$

4. $4 \times 4 \times 4 \times 4 \times 4 \times 4 \times 4 \times 4$

Write each expression in standard form.

5. $(0.5)^3$

6. $(2.7)^2$

7. 2^3

8. $(8.1)^3$

Write each number in scientific notation.

9. 480,000

10. 960,000

11. 8,750,000

12. 407,000

Name ______________________ Date ____________ Class ____________

Additional Practice

1. A bathtub is being filled at a rate of 2.5 gallons per minute. The bathtub will hold 20 gallons of water.

   a. How long will it take to fill the bathtub?

   b. Is the relationship described linear, inverse, exponential, or neither? Write an equation relating the variables.

2. Suppose a single bacterium lands on one of your teeth and starts reproducing by a factor of 4 every hour.

   a. After how many hours will there be at least 1,000,000 bacteria in the new colony?

   b. Is the relationship described linear, inverse, exponential, or neither? Write an equation relating the variables.

3. Two students who work in a grocery store are making a display of canned goods. They build a tower of cans 12 layers deep. The first layer, at the top, contains three cans in a row. The second layer contains six cans, in two rows of three that support the first layer. The third layer has nine cans, in three rows of three that support the second layer.

   a. How many cans are in layer 12, the bottom layer?

   b. Is the relationship described linear, inverse, exponential, or neither? Write an equation relating the variables.

Name ______________________ Date __________ Class __________

Additional Practice *(continued)*

4. An experimental plant has an unusual growth pattern. On each day, the plant doubles its height of the previous day. On the first day of the experiment, the plant grows to twice, or 2 times, its original height. On the second day, the plant grows to 4 times its original height. On the third day, the plant grows to 8 times its original height.

a. How many times its original height does the plant reach on the sixth day? On the *n*th day?

b. If the plant is 128 cm tall on the ninth day, how tall was it just before the experiment began?

c. Is the relationship described linear, inverse, exponential, or neither? Write an equation relating the variables.

Study the pattern in each table. Tell whether the relationship between x and y is linear, inverse, exponential, or neither, and explain your reasoning. If the relationship is linear, inverse, or exponential, write an equation for it.

5.

x	0	1	2	3	4	5
y	2	9	16	23	30	37

6.

x	0	1	2	3	4	5
y	2	4	8	16	32	64

7.

x	0	1	2	3	4	5
y	$\frac{1}{16}$	$\frac{1}{4}$	1	4	16	64

8.

x	0	1	2	3	4	5
y	1	$\frac{1}{2}$	$\frac{1}{3}$	$\frac{1}{4}$	$\frac{1}{5}$	$\frac{1}{6}$

9.

x	0	1	2	3	4	5
y	1	14	116	614	2,156	10,124

Name ______________________ Date ____________ Class ____________

Skill: Exponential Functions

Investigation 2

Growing, Growing, Growing

Complete the table for each exercise.

1. Investment increases by 1.5 times every 5 yr.

Time	Value of Investment
Initial	$800
5 yr	$1200
10 yr	$1800
15 yr	$2700
20 yr	
25 yr	

2. The number of animals doubles every 3 mo.

Time	Number of Animals
Initial	18
3 mo	36
6 mo	72
9 mo	
12 mo	

3. The amount of matter doubles every 6 months.

Time	Amount of Matter
Initial	10 g
1 yr	40 g
2 yr	160 g
3 yr	
4 yr	

Skill: Exponential Functions *(continued)*

Graph each function.

4. $y = 3^x$

5. $y = 10 \cdot 5^x$

6. $y = \frac{1}{8} \cdot 2^x$

Additional Practice

1. Suppose you deposit $1,000 in a savings account that earns interest of 6% per year on the current balance in the account.
   a. If you leave your money in the account for 10 years, what will the value of your investment be at the end of the 10 years?

   b. Write an equation relating the variables.

2. Janelle deposits $2,000 in the bank. The bank will pay 5% interest per year, compounded annually. This means that Janelle's money will grow by 5% each year.
   a. Make a table showing Janelle's balance at the end of each year for 5 years.

   b. Write an equation for calculating the balance b at the end of any year t.

   c. Approximately how many years will it take for the original deposit to double in value? Explain your reasoning.

   d. Suppose the interest rate is 10%. Approximately how many years will it take for the original deposit to double in value? How does this interest rate compare with an interest rate of 5%?

Additional Practice *(continued)*

For Exercises 3–6, tell whether the relationship between *x* and *y* is linear, inverse, exponential, or neither, and explain your answer. If the relationship is linear, inverse, or exponential, write an equation for the relationship.

3.

x	0	1	2	3	4	5
y	2	2.6	3.38	4.394	5.7122	7.42586

4.

x	0	1	2	3	4	5
y	500	550	605	665.5	732.05	805.255

5.

x	0	1	2	3	4	5
y	2.3	3.8	5.3	6.8	8.3	9.8

6.

x	1	2	3	4	5
y	$\frac{1}{2}$	$\frac{1}{4}$	$\frac{1}{6}$	$\frac{1}{8}$	$\frac{1}{10}$

7. Consider these three equations: $y = 5^x$, $y = 3^x$, and $y = 1 + 10^x$.

a. Sketch graphs of the equations on one set of axes.

b. What points, if any, do the three graphs have in common?

c. In which graph does the *y*-value increase at the greatest rate as the *x*-value increases?

d. Use the graphs to figure out which of the equations is not an example of exponential growth.

e. Use the equations to figure out which is not an example of exponential growth.

Name ______________________ Date __________ Class __________

Skill: Compound Interest

Investigation 3

Growing, Growing, Growing

For Exercises 1–2, complete each table. Compound the interest annually.

1. $5,000 at 6% for 4 years.

Principal at Beginning of Year	Interest	Balance
Year 1: $5,000		
Year 2:		
Year 3:		
Year 4:		

2. $7,200 at 3% for 4 years

Principal at Beginning of Year	Interest	Balance
Year 1: $7,200		
Year 2:		
Year 3:		
Year 4:		

3. Suppose one of your ancestors invested $500 in 1800 in an account paying 4% interest compounded annually. Write an exponential function to model the situation. Find the account balance in each of the following years.

a. 1850

b. 1900

c. 2000

d. 2100

Additional Practice

1. Joan and Jeff are standing 50 meters apart. They take turns walking toward each other. Jeff walks one half the distance between them, then Joan walks one half the distance between them. They take turns, each walking one half the remaining distance between them. Suppose that each walks 4 times (8 rounds) during this exercise.

   a. Make a table showing how far apart Joan and Jeff are after each of the first 8 rounds.

   b. Make a graph of your data from part (a).

   c. Suppose that Joan and Jeff start over and take turns walking 3 feet toward each other. Make a table and a graph for this walking exercise showing how far apart they will be after each of the first 8 rounds.

   d. Compare the tables and graphs for the two situations. Explain the similarities and the differences you see.

Additional Practice *(continued)*

2. A tree farm has begun to harvest a section of trees that was planted a number of years ago.

Supply of Trees

Year	0	1	2	3	4	5	6	7	8
Trees Remaining	10,000	9,502	9,026	8,574	8,145	7,737	7,350	6,892	6,543

a. Suppose the relationship between the year and the trees remaining is exponential. Approximate the decay factor for this relationship.

b. Write an equation for the relationship between time and trees remaining.

c. Evaluate your equation for each of the years shown in the table below to find the approximate number of trees remaining.

Supply of Trees

Year	10	15	20	25	30	35	40
Trees Remaining							

d. The owners of the farm intend to stop harvesting when only 15% of the trees remain. During which year will this occur? Explain your reasoning.

Name ______________________________ Date ____________ Class ____________

Additional Practice *(continued)*

3. Kai's brother collects fuzzy insects called tribetts. The tribett population decreases by 30% each year.

a. Make a table showing the number of tribetts at the end of the first 5 years for a starting population of 10,000 tribetts.

Tribett Population

Year	0	1	2	3	4	5
Tribetts						

b. Write an equation for the relationship between years and number of tribetts.

c. In what year will there first be fewer than 1,000 tribetts?

4. There are 64 volleyball teams entered in the state competition. In the first round of play, each team plays one other team, so 32 games will be played in the single elimination tournament. The winners from these games play each other in a second round. The winners of the second round play each other in a third round. This continues until there is a final winning team. There are no tie games; games are played into overtime if needed.

a. How many rounds of play are needed before a winner is determined? Explain your reasoning.

b. How many total games are played before a winner is determined? Explain.

c. Suppose an additional round of play is added to the playoffs. How many teams would start in the playoffs? Explain.

Name ______________________ Date ____________ Class ____________

Skill: Exponential Growth and Decay

Investigation 4

Growing, Growing, Growing

1. Complete the table for integer values of x from 0 to 4. Then graph the function.

$y = 50(0.2)^x$

x	y	(x, y)
0		
1		
2		
3		
4		

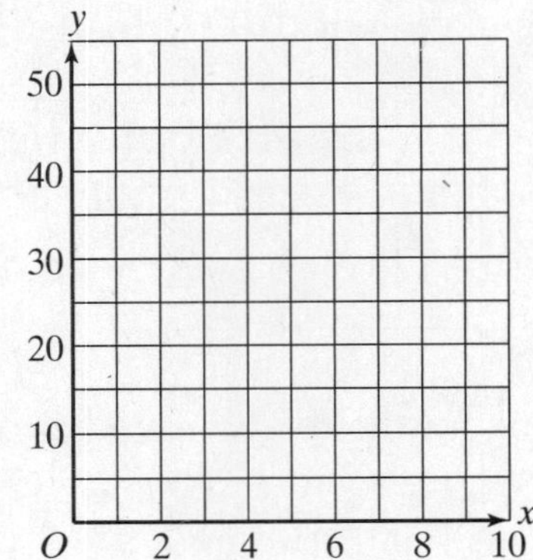

Write an exponential function to model each situation. Find each amount after the specified time.

2. Suppose the acreage of forest is decreasing by 2% per year because of development. If there are currently 4,500,000 acres of forest, determine the amount of forest land after each of the following.

a. 3 years **b.** 5 years **c.** 10 years **d.** 20 years

3. A \$10,500 investment has a 15% loss each year. Determine the value of the investment after each of the following.

a. 1 year **b.** 2 years **c.** 4 years **d.** 10 years

4. A city of 2,950,000 people has a 2.5% annual decrease in population. Determine the city's population after each of the following.

a. 1 year **b.** 5 years **c.** 15 years **d.** 25 years

5. A \$25,000 purchase decreases 12% in value per year. Determine the value of the purchase after each of the following.

a. 1 year **b.** 3 years **c.** 5 years **d.** 7 years

Name ______________________________ Date ____________ Class ____________

Additional Practice

Investigation 5

Growing, Growing, Growing

1. In parts (a)–(f), write the expression in an equivalent form using exponents. Then write the expression in standard form.

   a. $2^5 \times 2^5$

   b. $4^3 \times 2^5$

   c. 25^4

   d. $\frac{3^4}{3}$

   e. $10^2 \times 2 \times 5$

   f. $3^3 \times 2^3$

2. In parts (a)–(d), find the units digit of the standard form of the expression.

   a. 12^{10}

   b. 11^{23}

   c. 23^{19}

   d. 17^{17}

3. Consider these three equations: $y = 0.625^x$, $y = 0.375^x$, and $y = 1 - 0.5x$.

   a. Sketch graphs of the equations on one set of axes.

   b. What points, if any, do the three graphs have in common?

   c. In which graph does the y-value decrease at a faster and faster rate as the x-value increases?

4. Decide whether each statement is true or false. Explain your reasoning.

   a. $3^5 + 3^5 = 3^{10}$

   b. $5^4 + 2^4 = 7^4$

Name ____________________ Date __________ Class __________

Skill: Simplifying Exponential Expressions

Investigation 5

Growing, Growing, Growing

Find an equivalent expression.

1. $3^2 \cdot 3^5$

2. $1^3 \cdot 1^4$

3. $5^4 \cdot 5^3$

4. $4.5^8 \cdot 4.5^2$

5. $3^3 \cdot 3 \cdot 3^4$

Replace each $\square$ with =, <, or >.

6. $3^8 \square 3 \cdot 3^7$

7. $49 \square 7^2 \cdot 7^2$

8. $5^3 \cdot 5^4 \square 25^2$

Simplify each expression.

9. $\frac{(-3)^6}{(-3)^8}$

10. $\frac{8^4}{8^0}$

11. $\frac{(-4)^8}{(-4)^4}$

12. $\frac{7^5}{7^3}$

13. $\frac{(-3)^5}{(-3)^8}$

Name ______________________ Date ____________ Class ____________

Additional Practice

Investigation 1

Frogs, Fleas, and Painted Cubes

1. The area A of a rectangle with a side of length ℓ meters and a fixed perimeter is given by the equation $A = \ell(240 - \ell)$.

   a. Suppose one dimension of the rectangle is 180 meters. What is the other dimension? What is the area of the rectangle?

   b. Suppose one dimension of the rectangle is 110 meters. What is the other dimension? What is the area of the rectangle?

   c. What are the dimensions of the rectangle with the greatest area possible for this perimeter? Explain how you found your answer.

   d. What are the dimensions of the rectangle with this perimeter and an area of 8,000 square meters? Explain your answer.

   e. What is the fixed perimeter for the rectangles represented by this equation? Explain how you found the perimeter.

2. The graph shows length and area data for rectangles with a fixed perimeter.

   a. What are the dimensions of the rectangle with this perimeter and an area of 8 square meters?

   b. What are the dimensions of the rectangle with this perimeter and an area of 5 square meters?

   c. What is the greatest area possible for a rectangle with this perimeter? What are the dimensions of this rectangle?

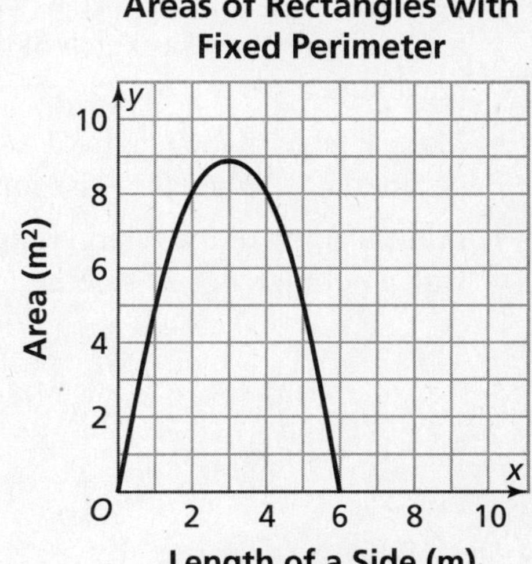

Additional Practice *(continued)*

3. Find the maximum area for a rectangle with a perimeter of 10 meters. Include the following in your answer and explain how each piece of evidence supports your answer:

- Sketches of rectangles with a perimeter of 10 meters that do not have the maximum area and a sketch of the rectangle you think does have the maximum area.
- Make a table of the length of a side and the area for rectangles with a perimeter of 10 meters. Use increments of 1 meter for the lengths.
- Make a graph of the relationship between length and area of rectangles with a perimeter of 10 meters.

4. Find the maximum area for a rectangle with a perimeter of 200 meters. Include the following in your answer and explain how each piece of evidence supports your answer:

- Sketches of rectangles with a perimeter of 200 meters that do not have the maximum area and a sketch of the rectangle you think does have the maximum area.
- Make a table of the length of a side and the area for rectangles with a perimeter of 200 meters. Use increments of 10 meters for the lengths.
- Make a graph of the relationship between length and area of rectangles with a perimeter of 200 meters.

Additional Practice *(continued)*

5. The rectangle below has a perimeter of 60 meters and a side length ℓ meters.

?

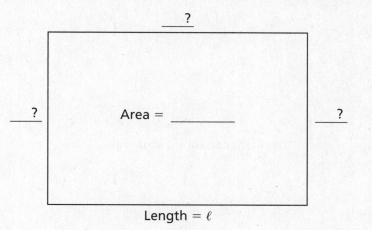

? Area = ________ ?

Length = ℓ

a. Express the lengths of the other sides in terms of ℓ.

b. Write an equation for the Area A in terms of ℓ.

c. Make a graph of your equation.

d. Use your equation to find the area of the rectangle if the length of one side is 10 meters.

e. Describe how you could use your graph to find the area of the rectangle if the length of one side is 10 meters.

f. Describe how you could use a table to find the area of the rectangle if the length of one side is 10 meters.

g. What is the maximum area possible for a rectangle with a perimeter of 60 meters? What are the dimensions of the rectangle with maximum area?

Additional Practice *(continued)*

6. a. Use your results to Exercises 3–5 above to describe the shape of a rectangle with maximum area.

b. What are the dimensions of a rectangle with maximum area if the perimeter is 100 meters?

c. What are the dimensions of a rectangle with maximum area if the perimeter is 10 meters?

d. What are the dimensions of a rectangle with maximum area if the perimeter is 1 meter?

e. What are the dimensions of a rectangle with maximum area if the perimeter is 0.1 meter?

Name ______________________ Date ____________ Class ____________

Additional Practice

Investigation 2

Frogs, Fleas, and Painted Cubes

1. Refer to the diagram below to answer parts (a)–(f).

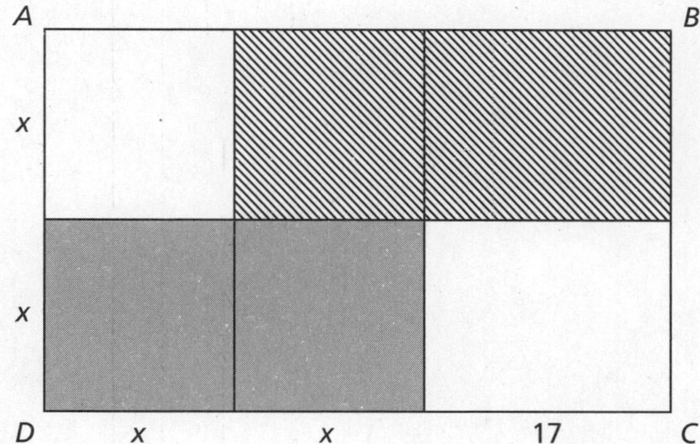

a. Write an expression for the area of the diagonally shaded region.

b. Write an expression for the area of the gray region.

c. Write an expression for the total area of the white regions.

d. Write an expression for the difference in areas between the diagonally shaded region and the gray region.

e. Write an expression for the perimeter of rectangle *ABCD*.

f. Write an expression for the area of rectangle *ABCD*.

Draw and label a rectangle whose area is represented by the expression. Then write an equivalent expression in expanded form.

2. $(x + 1)(x + 5)$ **3.** $3x(x - 4)$ **4.** $(x + 6)(x + 2)$

Additional Practice *(continued)*

For Exercises 5–10, write the expression in factored form. You may want to draw a rectangle to illustrate the area represented by the expression.

5. $x^2 + 2x + 9x + 18$

6. $x^2 + 4x$

7. $x^2 + 12x + 36$

8. $x^2 + 2x + 7x + 14$

9. $x^2 + 7x + 12$

10. $x^2 + 12x + 27$

11. Serena and Chuck had a large square piece of cardboard for designing a poster advertising the upcoming drama club fund-raiser. They decided to trim 3 feet from the length of the cardboard.

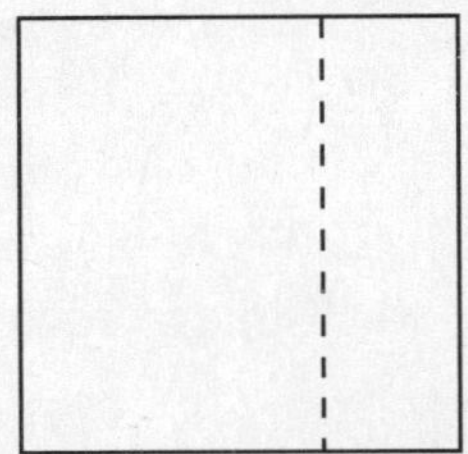

Suppose each side of the original square of cardboard had a length of x feet.

a. Write an expression for the area of the strip that Serena and Chuck trimmed from the large piece.

b. Write an expression for the area of the remaining piece of cardboard.

c. Write an expression for the perimeter of the strip that Serena and Chuck trimmed from the large piece.

d. Write an expression for the perimeter of the remaining piece of cardboard.

e. The perimeter of the original piece of cardboard was 36 feet.

i. What is the area of the strip that Serena and Chuck trimmed from the large piece?

ii. What is the area of the remaining piece of cardboard?

iii. What is the perimeter of the remaining piece of cardboard?

Additional Practice *(continued)*

12. A square has sides of length x centimeters. A new rectangle is made by increasing one dimension by 2 centimeters and decreasing the other dimension by 2 centimeters.

a. Make a table showing the area of the square and the area of the new rectangle for whole number x values from 0 to 10.

b. Which values for area are not reasonable? Explain.

c. On the same set of axes, graph the (x, area) data for both the square and the rectangle. Graph only those values for which the area is positive.

d. Write an equation for the area of the original square and an equation for the area of the new rectangle. Use these equations to label the graphs you made in part (c).

13. A square has sides of length x centimeters. A new rectangle is made by increasing one dimension by 2 centimeters.

a. Make a sketch to show how the square is transformed into the new rectangle.

b. Make a table showing the area of the square and the area of the new rectangle for whole number x values from 0 to 10.

c. On the same set of axes, graph the (x, area) data for both the square and the rectangle.

d. Write an equation for the area of the original square and an equation for the area of the new rectangle.

Name ______________________ Date __________ Class __________

Additional Practice *(continued)*

Write two expressions, one in factored form and one in expanded form, for the area of the unshaded region.

14.

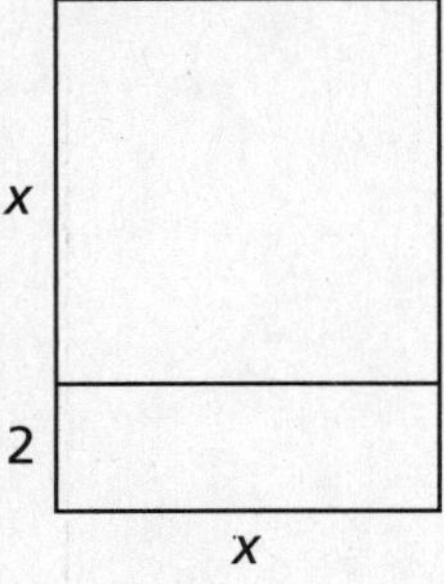

15.

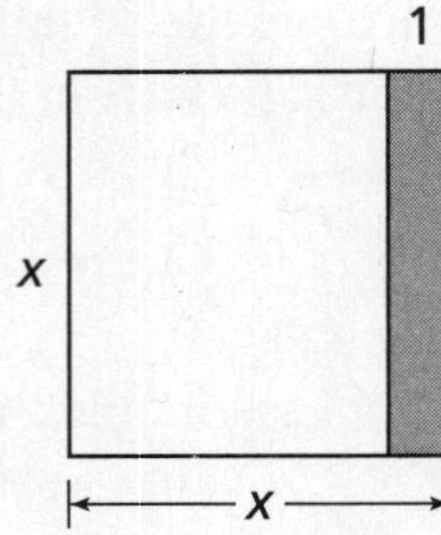

16.

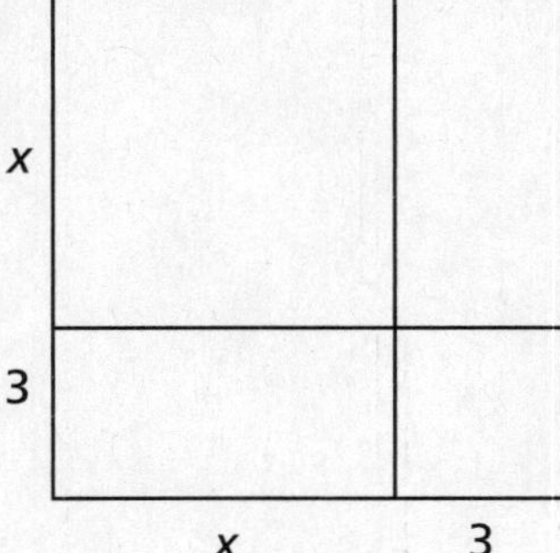

17.

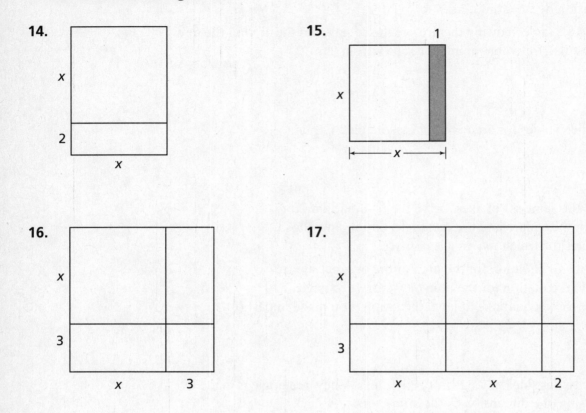

For Exercises 18–21, draw and label a rectangle whose area is represented by the expression. Write an equivalent expression in factored form.

18. $x^2 + 4x$

19. $x^2 + x + x + 1$

20. $x^2 + 3x + 2$

21. $x^2 + 2x + 1$

Name ______________________ Date ____________ Class ____________

Skill: Writing Expressions in Expanded Form

Investigation 2

Frogs, Fleas, and Painted Cubes

Find the area of each rectangle.

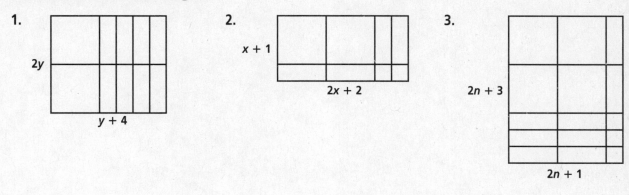

1.

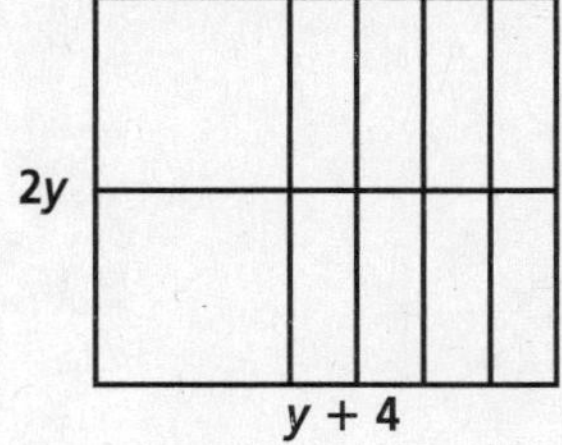

2.

x + 1

2x + 2

3.

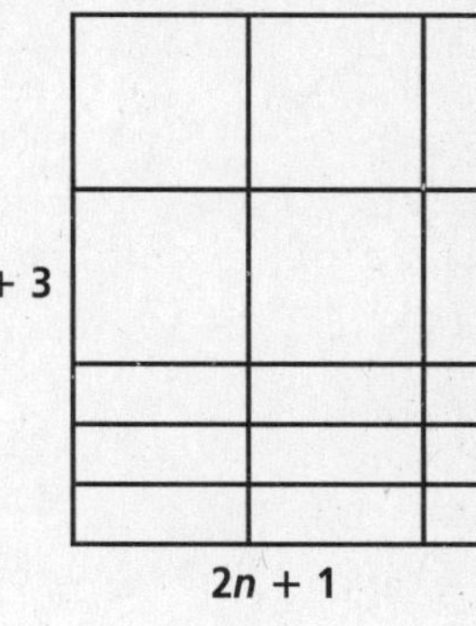

Use the Distributive Property to write each expression in expanded form.

4. $x(x+2)$

5. $3b(b-5)$

6. $2x^2(x+9)$

7. $2(a^2+8a+1)$

8. $2x^2(4x+1)$

9. $3l(l^2+4l-6)$

10. $(x+2)(x+3)$

11. $(x+5)(x+1)$

12. $(x+4)(x+5)$

13. $(x+7)(x+2)$

14. $(x+1)(x-6)$

15. $(x+8)(x-3)$

Skill: Factoring Expressions

Use the Distributive Property to factor each expression.

1. $x^2+8x+16$

2. d^2+8d+7

3. y^2+6y+8

4. b^2-2b-3

5. s^2-4s-5

6. $x^2+12x+32$

7. $x^2-9x+20$

8. x^2-5x+6

9. a^2+3a+2

10. p^2-8p+7

11. d^2+6d+5

12. n^2+n-6

13. $x(a-2)-2(a+2)$

14. $3(x+y) + a(x+y)$

15. $m(x-3) - k(x-3)$

Name ______________________________ Date ____________ Class ____________

Skill: Graphs of Parabolas

Graph each function. Label the axis of symmetry, the vertex, and the y-intercept.

1. $y = x^2 - 6x + 4$

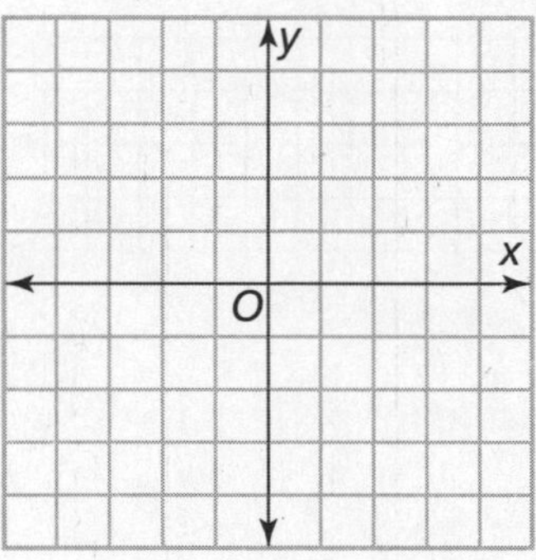

2. $y = x^2 + 4x - 1$

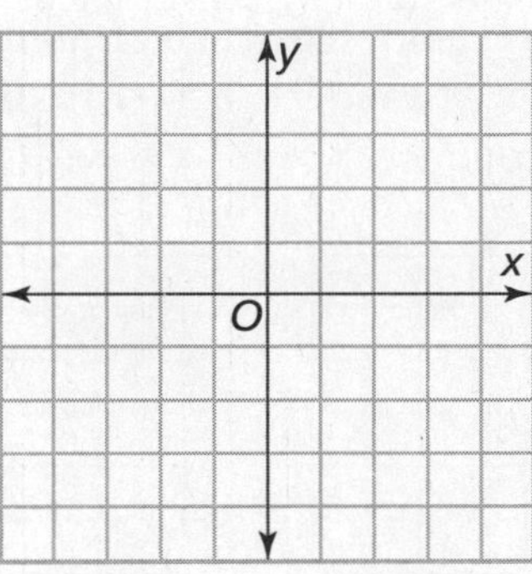

3. $y = x^2 + 10x + 14$

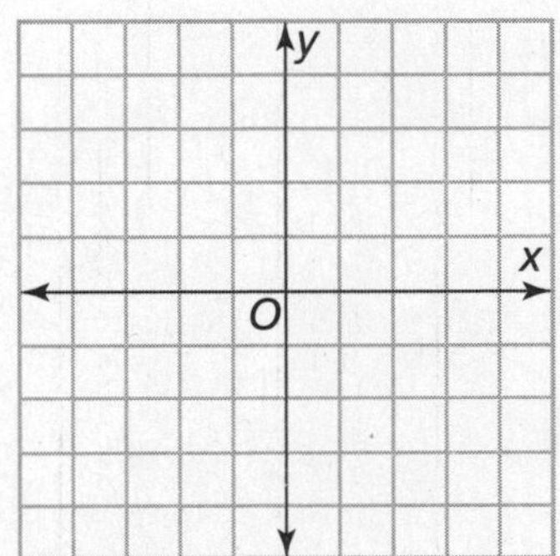

Name ______________________________ Date ____________ Class ____________

Additional Practice

1. a. The pattern below represents a sequence of squares arranged as rectangles. How many squares are in the next two rectangles?

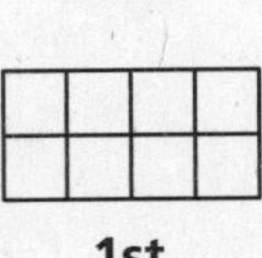

1st

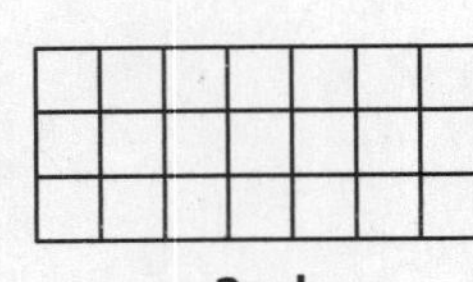

2nd

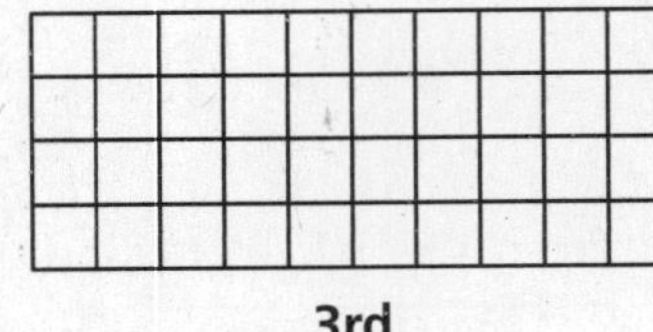

3rd

b. Describe the pattern of change from one rectangular pattern to the next.

c. Use the pattern of change you have described to predict the total number of squares in the 6th and 7th figure in the sequence.

d. Which equation below can be used to find the total number of squares c in the nth rectangle?

$c = (n + 1)(n + 3)$ $c = (n + 1)(3n + 1)$ $c = n + 1(3n + 1)$

2. a. The unshaded squares in the grids below represent a sequence of numbers. The first three numbers in the sequence are 99, 96, and 91. What are the next two numbers to be represented in the sequence?

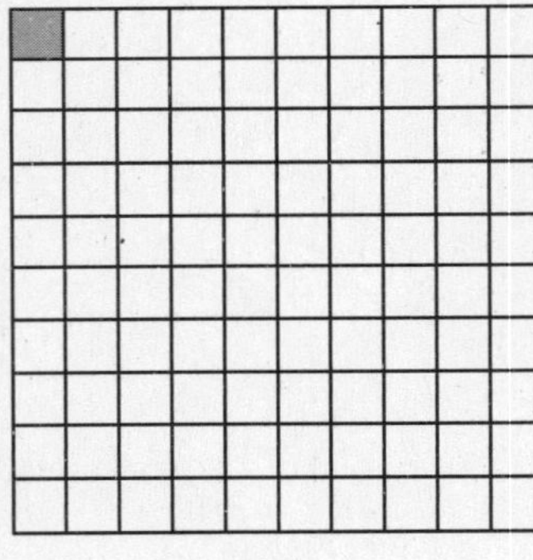

1st

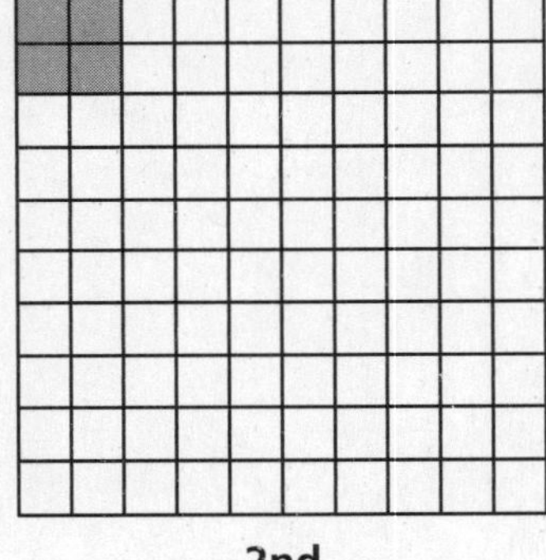

2nd

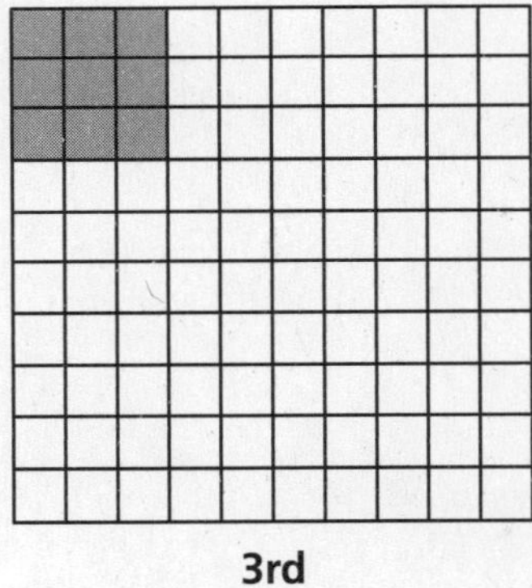

3rd

b. Describe the pattern of change from one grid to the next.

c. Use the pattern of change you have described to predict the 6th and 7th numbers in the sequence.

d. Write an equation for calculating the nth number in the sequence.

e. This sequence of numbers is an example of a *finite sequence*, which means that the sequence does not go on forever but eventually comes to an end. How many numbers are in the sequence? Explain your reasoning.

Name ______________________ Date __________ Class __________

Additional Practice *(continued)*

3. a. Study the number sequence: 1×3, 2×4, 3×5, 4×6, 5×7, 6×8. What are the next two numbers in the sequence?

b. Describe how you might calculate the *n*th number in the sequence.

c. Write an equation for calculating the *n*th number in the sequence.

d. Make a table and a graph of the first ten numbers in this sequence. Describe the pattern of change from one number to the next.

4. a. The pattern of squares below represent the first four numbers in a sequence. What are the total number of squares in the next two figures?

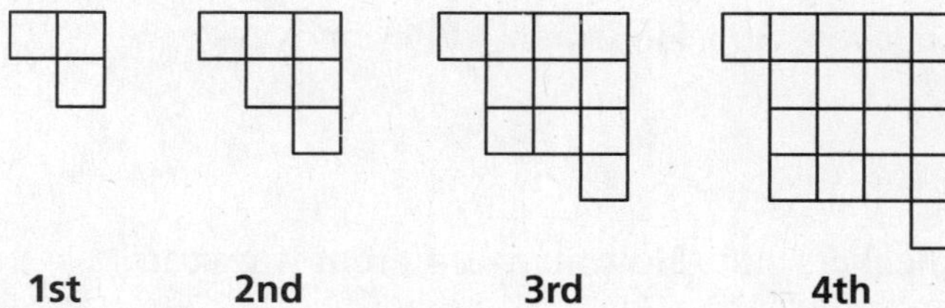

1st 2nd 3rd 4th

b. Describe the arrangement of squares representing the *n*th figure in the sequence.

c. Write an equation for calculating the number of squares *s* in the *n*th figure in the sequence.

d. Make a table and a graph of the total number of squares in the first ten figures in this sequence. Describe the pattern of change from the number of squares in one figure to the next in the sequence.

Additional Practice *(continued)*

5. There are 6 students in the tennis club going to a tournament. How many different ways can they form doubles teams?

6. There are 6 students in the chess club. How many different ways can they play against each other?

7. There are 6 students planning a school dance. How many different committees of two members can they form?

8. What do you notice about your answers to Exercises 5, 6, and 7? Explain.

9. a. There are 2 students in the checkers club. How many different ways can they play against each other?

b. There are 3 students in the checkers club. How many different ways can they play against each other?

c. There are 4 students in the checkers club. How many different ways can they play against each other?

d. There are 5 students in the checkers club. How many different ways can they play against each other?

e. There are 6 students in the checkers club. How many different ways can they play against each other?

f. List the answers to parts (a) – (e). Describe the pattern of change from one answer to the next.

Name ______________________ Date ___________ Class ___________

Additional Practice

1. A ship conducting oceanographic research drops anchor offshore Honiara, the capitol of the Solomon Islands in the South Pacific. When the anchor is tossed into the water, the depth in feet D it has descended after t seconds is given by the equation $D = -4t^2 + 12t$.

   a. If it takes the anchor 10 seconds to reach the bottom, how deep is the water where the ship has dropped anchor?

   b. If the ship moves to another location and the anchor takes 8.5 seconds to reach the bottom, how deep is the water in that spot?

   c. If the ship anchors in the harbor of Honiara, where the water is 72 feet deep (that is, $D = -72$), how long will it take for the anchor to reach the bottom when it is dropped?

2. Metropolitan Container produces storage containers from recycled plastic. The total cost in dollars C of manufacturing n containers is given by the equation $C = 2n^2 + 9n + 100$.

   a. What is the total cost of manufacturing 4 containers?

   b. What is the total cost of manufacturing 10 containers?

   c. The *average cost* of manufacturing each container is $\frac{C}{n}$, the total cost of manufacturing the containers divided by the number of containers.

      i. Based on your answer to part (a), what is the average cost of manufacturing 4 containers?

      ii. Based on your answer to part (b), what is the average cost of manufacturing 10 containers?

iii. Compare your answers to parts (i) and (ii). What can you say about manufacturing 4 containers versus 10 containers?

d. The city of Metropolis has placed an order for a certain number of containers. If the cost of producing these containers is $3,660, how many containers did the city order? Explain your reasoning.

3. a. Complete this table for the equation $y = 5x^2$.

x	0	1	2	3	4
y					

b. What are the first differences in your table for the y values as x increases by 1?

c. What are the second differences in your table for the y values as x increases by 1?

d. Describe any patterns in the values you found in part (c) for the second differences.

4. a. Complete this table for the equation $y = 8x^2$.

x	0	1	2	3	4
y					

b. What are the first differences in your table for the y values as x increases by 1?

c. What are the second differences in your table for the y values as x increases by 1?

d. Describe any patterns in the values you found in part (c) for the second differences.

Name ______________________ Date __________ Class __________

5. a. Complete this table for the equation $y = 0.1x^2$.

x	0	1	2	3	4
y					

b. What are the first differences in your table for the y values as x increases by 1?

c. What are the second differences in your table for the y values as x increases by 1?

d. Describe any patterns in the values you found in part (c) for the second differences.

6. a. Complete this table for the equation $y = -3x^2$.

x	0	1	2	3	4
y					

b. What are the first differences in your table for the y values as x increases by 1?

c. What are the second differences in your table for the y values as x increases by 1?

d. Describe any patterns in the values you found in part (c) for the second differences.

7. Which of these are quadratic functions?

a. $y = x^2 - 7$ **b.** $y = 2(x + 7)$ **c.** $y = x(x + 7)$

d. $y = (x + 4)(x - 2)$ **e.** $y = (6 + 5)(x + 2)$ **f.** $y = (x - 3)(4)$

g. $y = 2x + 9$ **h.** $y = x^2 - 9$ **i.** $y = x + x + 9$

8. For each quadratic function in Exercise 7, find the coordinates of the x- and y-intercepts and the maximum/minimum point of the graph of the function.

Name ______________________ Date __________ Class __________

Skill: Quadratic Functions

Investigation 4

1. You and a friend are hiking in the mountains. You want to climb to a ledge that is 20 feet above you. The height of the grappling hook you throw is given by the function $h = -16t^2 - 32t + 5$. What is the maximum height of the grappling hook? Can you throw it high enough to reach the ledge?

2. The total profit made by an engineering firm is given by the function $p = x^2 - 25x + 5000$. Find the minimum profit made by the company.

3. You are trying to dunk a basketball. You need to jump 2.5 feet in the air to dunk the ball. The height that your feet are above the ground is given by the function $h = -16t^2 + 12t$. What is the maximum height your feet will be above the ground? Will you be able to dunk the basketball?

Name ______________________ Date ____________ Class ____________

Additional Practice

Investigation 1

Kaleidoscopes, Hubcaps, and Mirrors

Determine all the types of symmetry in the design. Specify lines of symmetry, centers and angles of rotation, and lengths and directions of translations.

1. 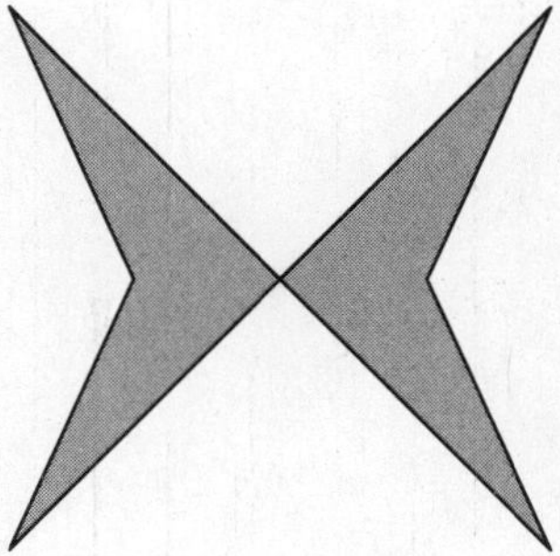

2. 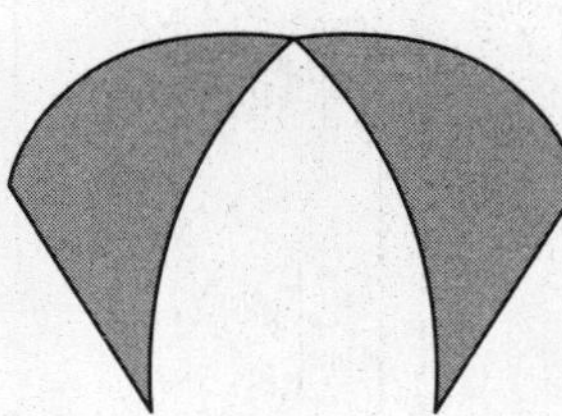

3. 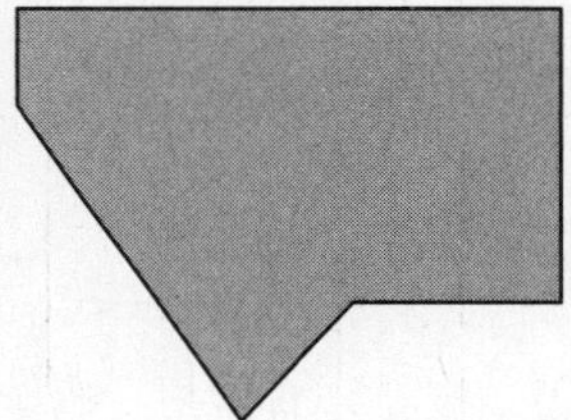

4. 

5. 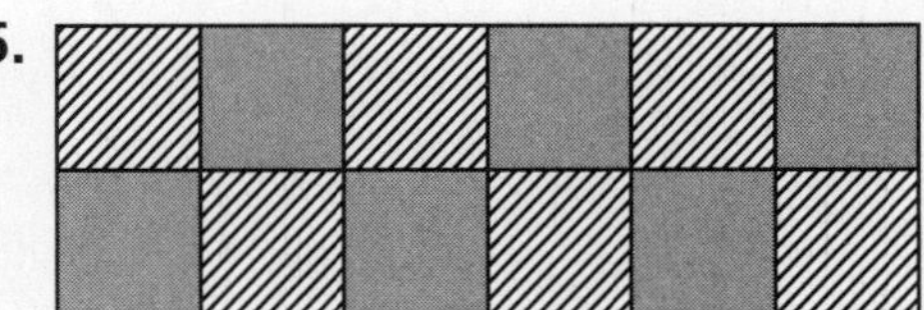

6. 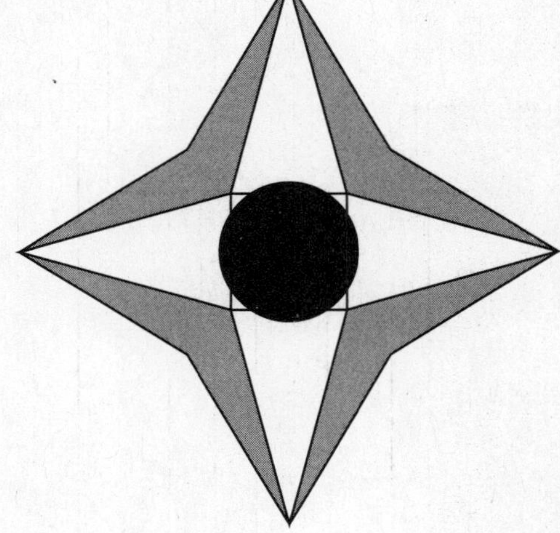

Additional Practice *(continued)*

A basic design element and one or more lines are given. Use the basic design element to create a design with the given lines as lines of symmetry.

7.

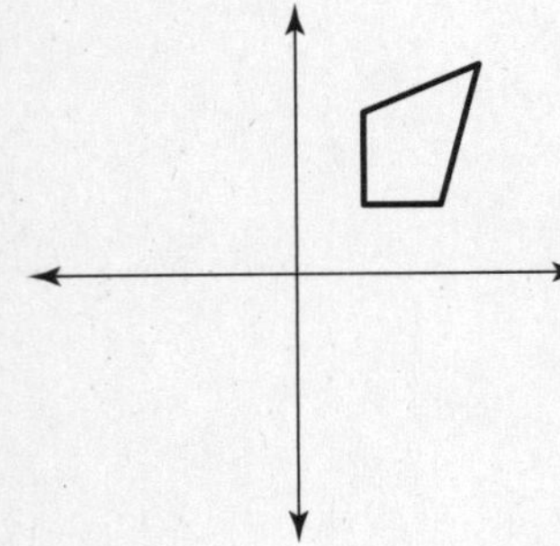

8.

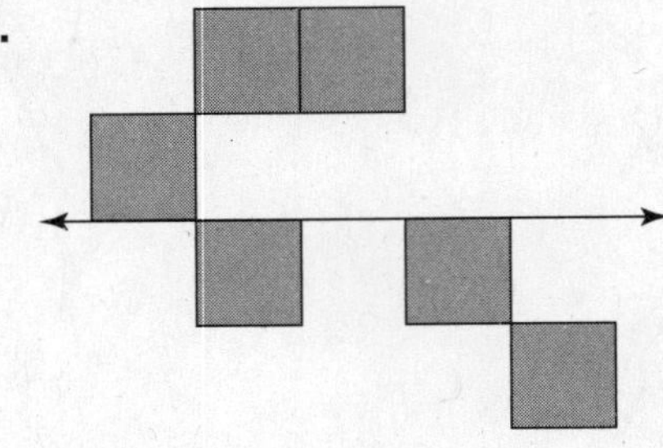

For Exercises 9–10, indicate the lines of symmetry and the center and angle of rotation for the design.

9.

10.

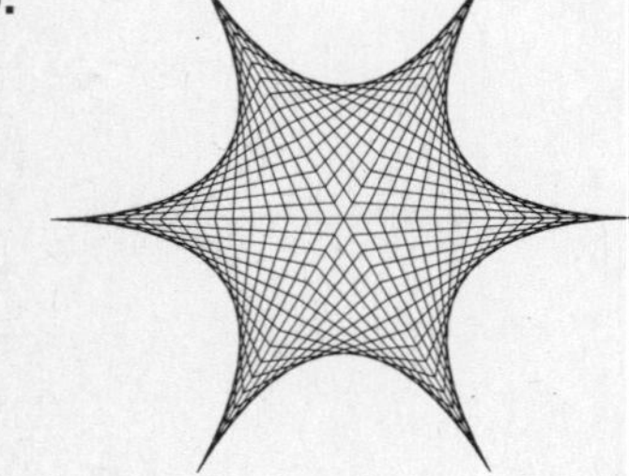

Name ______________________ Date ____________ Class ____________

Additional Practice *(continued)*

11. Using point P as a center of rotation, draw the image of the figure after a counterclockwise rotation of:

a. 90º

b. 180º

c. 270º

Name ________________ Date __________ Class __________

Skill: Identifying Reflection Symmetry

How many lines of symmetry can you find for each letter?

1. W **2.** X **3.** H **4.** T

Draw all the lines of symmetry for each figure.

5.

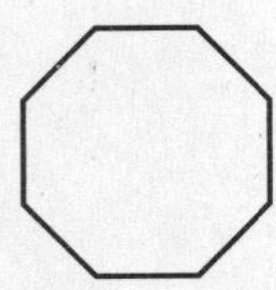

6.

7.

Is the dashed line a line of symmetry? Write yes or no.

8.

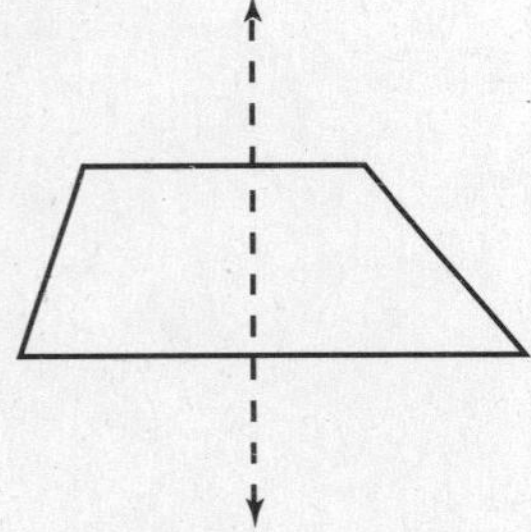

9.

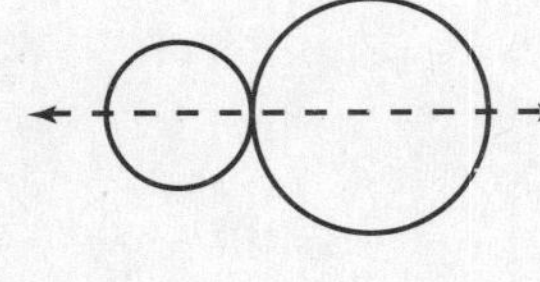

10.

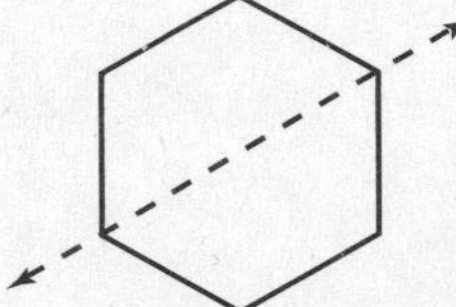

Name ______________________________ Date __________ Class __________

Skill: Identifying Rotation Symmetry

Investigation 1

Kaleidoscopes, Hubcaps, and Mirrors

Judging from appearances, does each figure have rotational symmetry? If yes, what is the angle of rotation?

1. 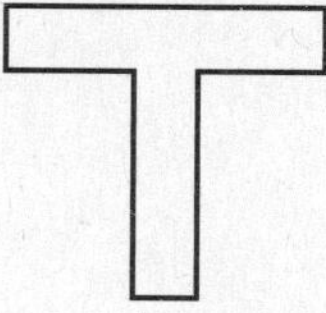

2. 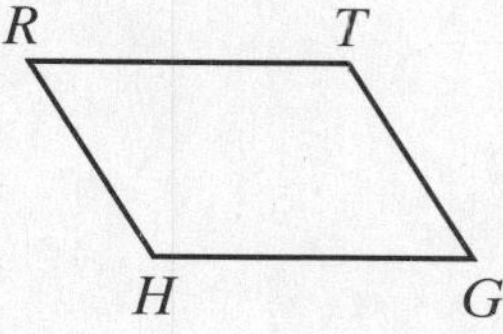

3. 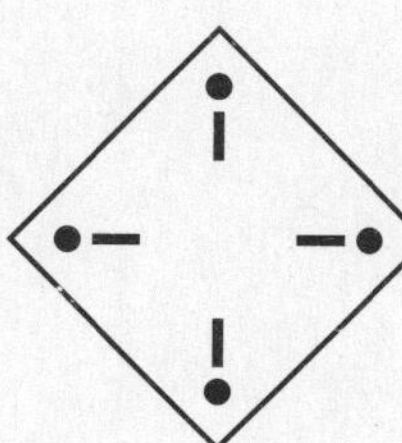

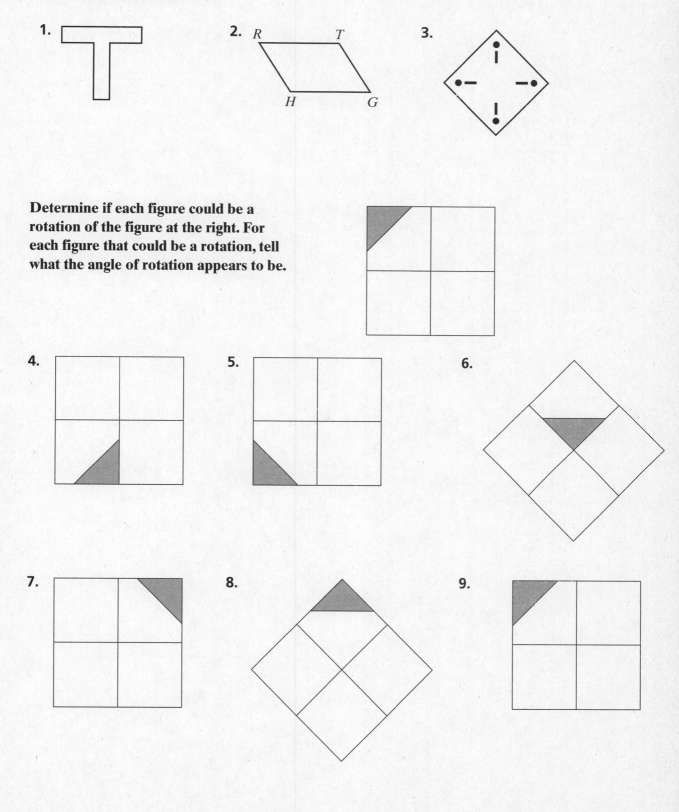

Determine if each figure could be a rotation of the figure at the right. For each figure that could be a rotation, tell what the angle of rotation appears to be.

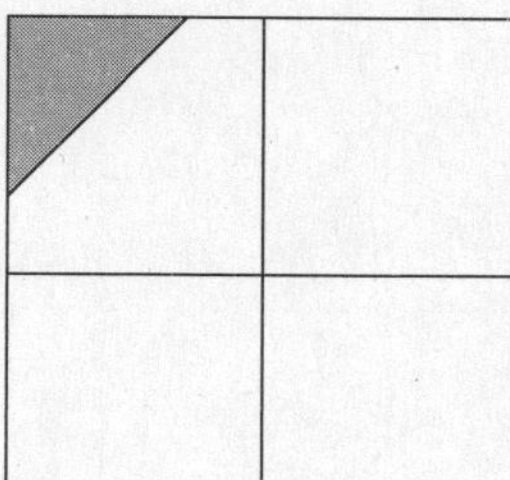

4. 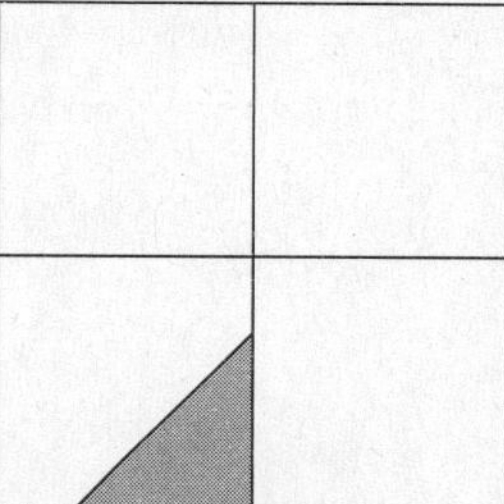

5. 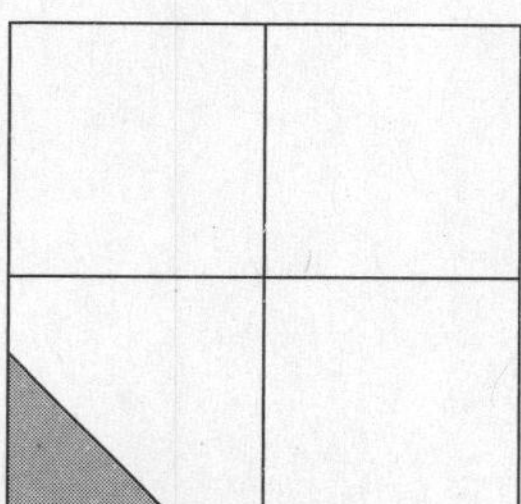

6. 

7. 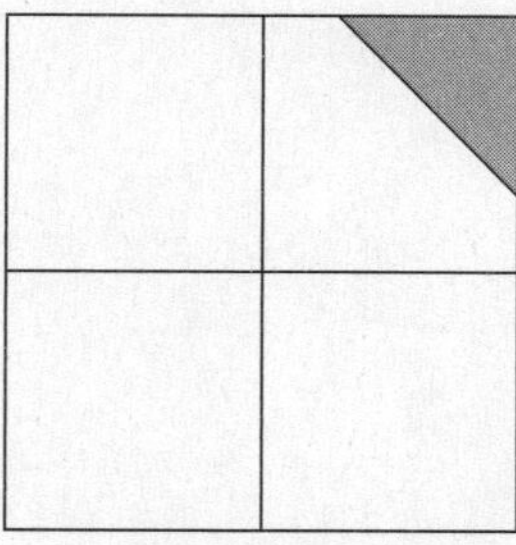

8. 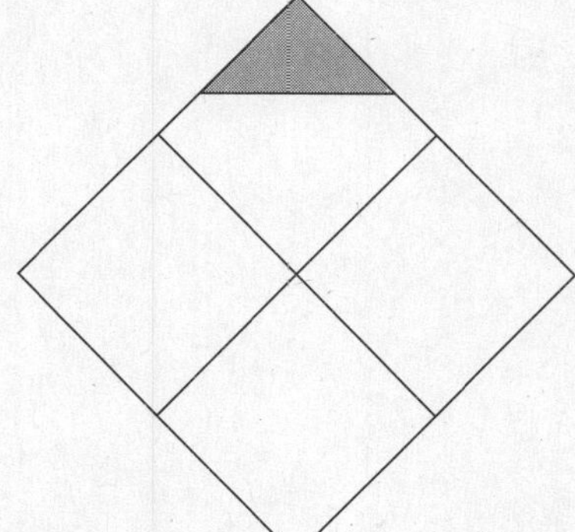

9. 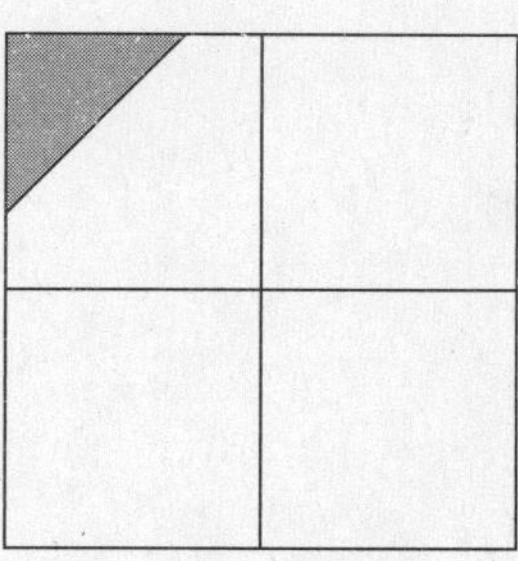

Additional Practice

Describe a reflection or a combination of two reflections that would move Shape 1 to exactly match Shape 2.

1.

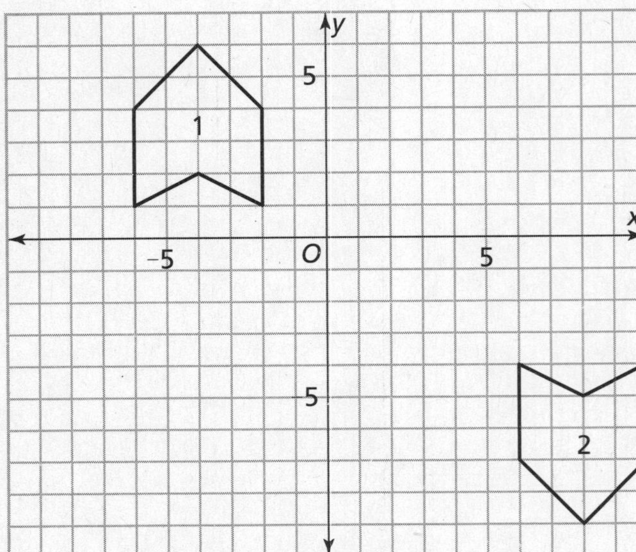

2.

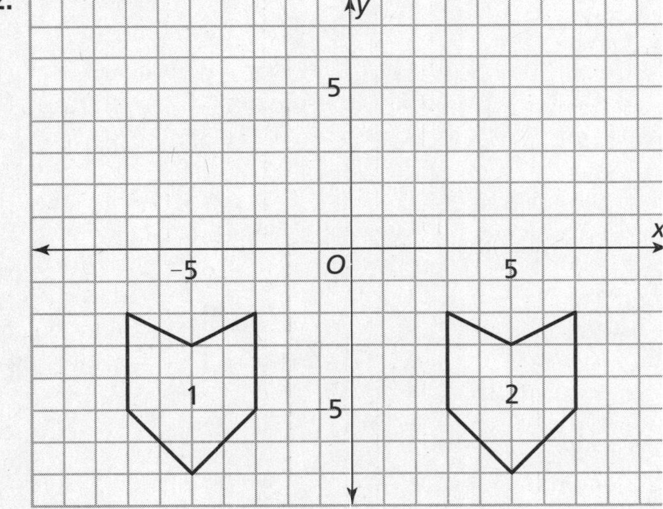

Name ______________________ Date __________ Class __________

Additional Practice *(continued)*

Draw the image of the polygon under a reflection in the line. Describe what happens to each point on the original polygon under the reflection.

3.

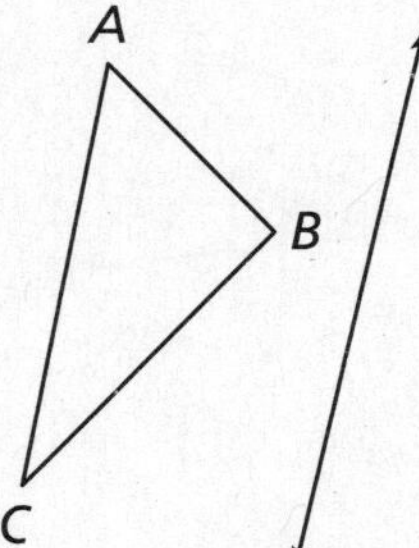

4.

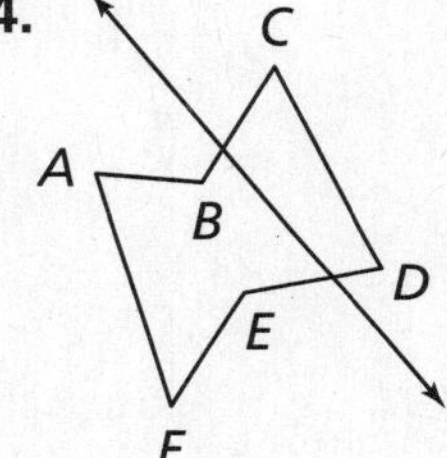

A shape and its image under a line reflection are given. Do parts (a) and (b).

a. Draw the line of symmetry for the figure.

b. Label three points on the figure, and label the corresponding image points.

5.

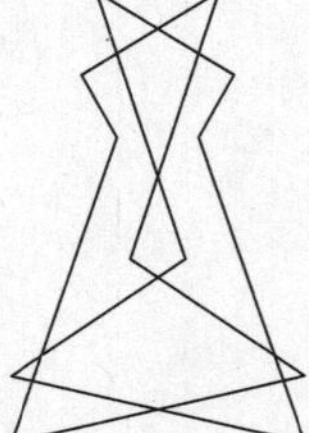

6.

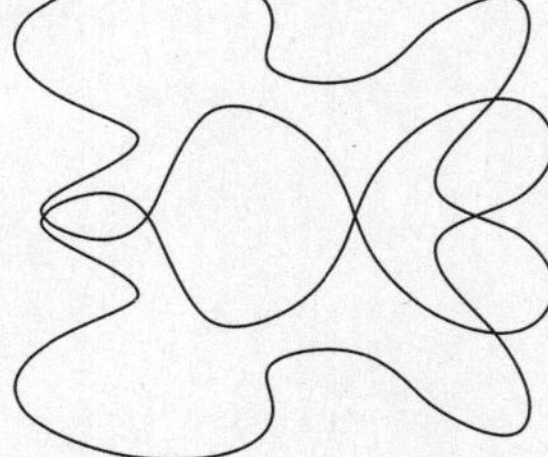

Additional Practice *(continued)*

For Exercises 7 and 8, perform the translation indicated by the arrow. Describe what happens to each point of the original figure under the translation.

7.

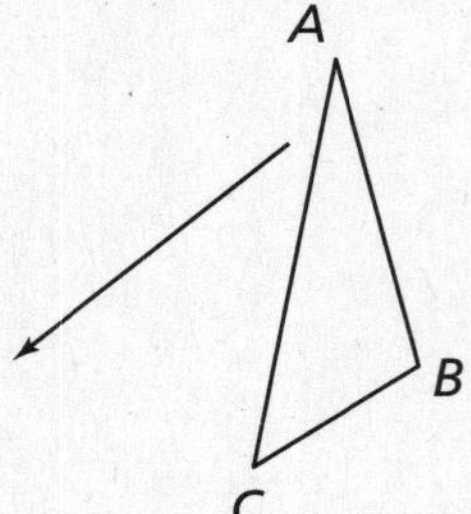

8.

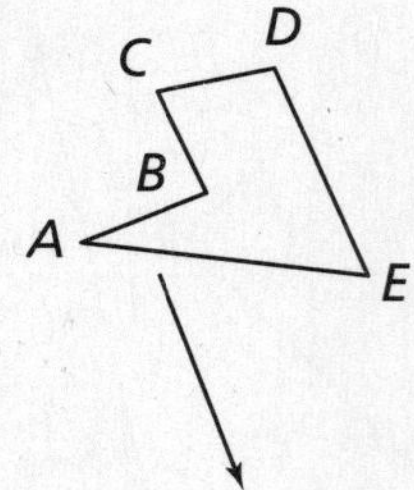

9. Rotate triangle *ABC* 90° *clockwise* about point *R*. Describe what happens to each point of triangle *ABC* under the rotation.

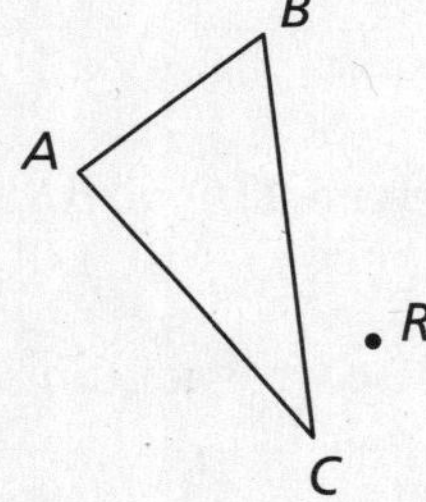

Name ______________________ Date ____________ Class ____________

10. Rotate polygon $ABCDEF$ 180° about point F. Describe what happens to each point of polygon $ABCDEF$ under the rotation.

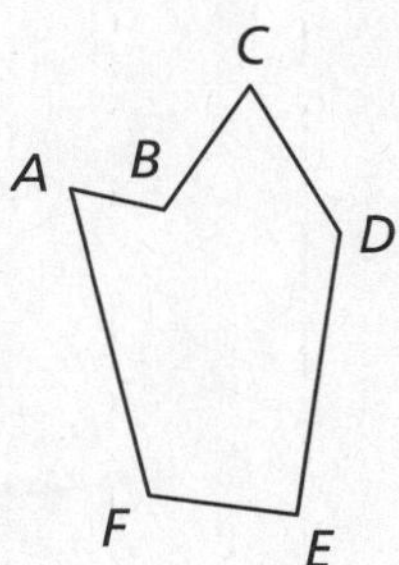

For Exercises 11-13, refer to this diagram.

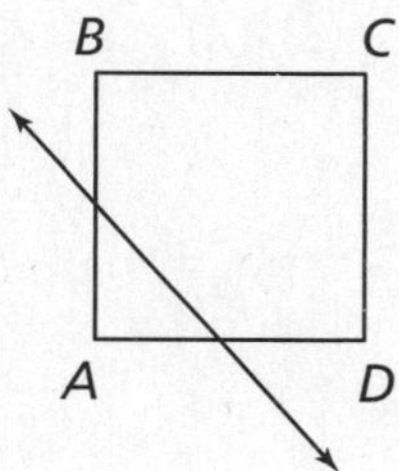

• P

11. Draw the image of square $ABCD$ under a reflection in the line.

12. Draw the image of square $ABCD$ under a 45° rotation about point D.

13. Draw the image of square $ABCD$ under the translation that slides point D to point P.

Additional Practice *(continued)*

For Exercises 14–17, a polygon and its image under a transformation are given. Decide whether the transformation was a line reflection, a rotation, or a translation. Then indicate the reflection line, the center and angle of rotation, or the direction and distance of the translation.

14.

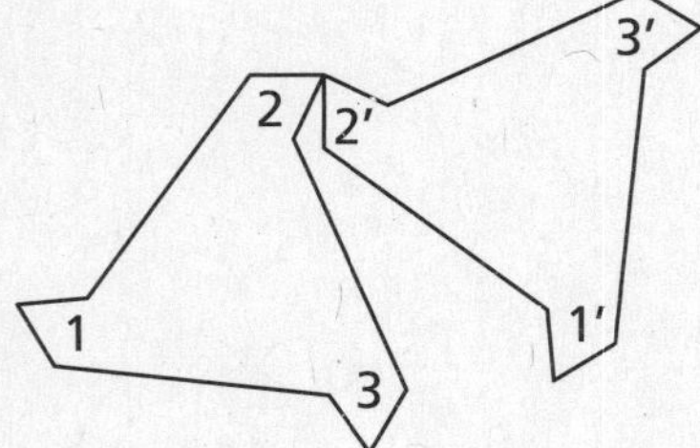

15.

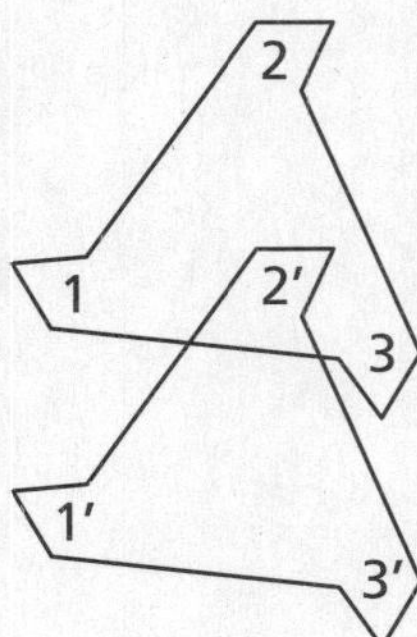

16.

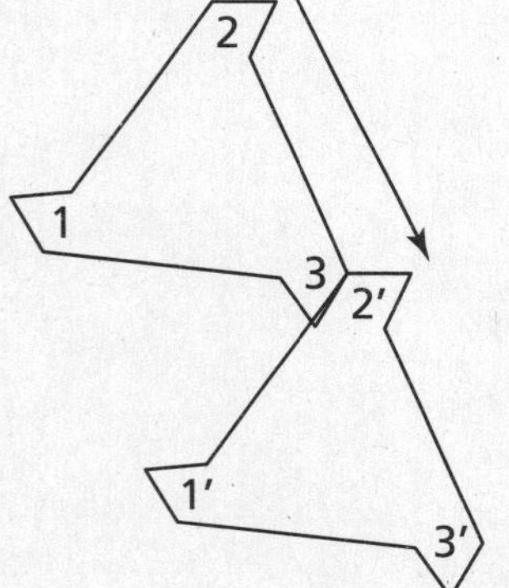

17.

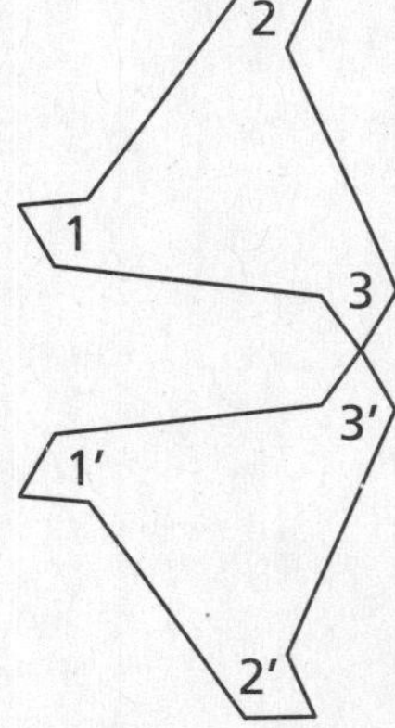

Additional Practice *(continued)*

18. Suppose the shape below is translated according to the rolls of a six-sided number cube.

- If a 1, 2, or 3 is rolled, the shape is translated 3 units to the right.
- If a 4 is rolled, the shape is translated 3 units up.
- If a 5 is rolled, the shape is translated 3 units down.
- If a 6 is rolled, the shape is translated 3 units to the left

a. Draw the shape in its location after the following sequence of rolls: 3, 5, 6. What are the new coordinates of a general point (x, y) on the shape after this sequence of rolls?

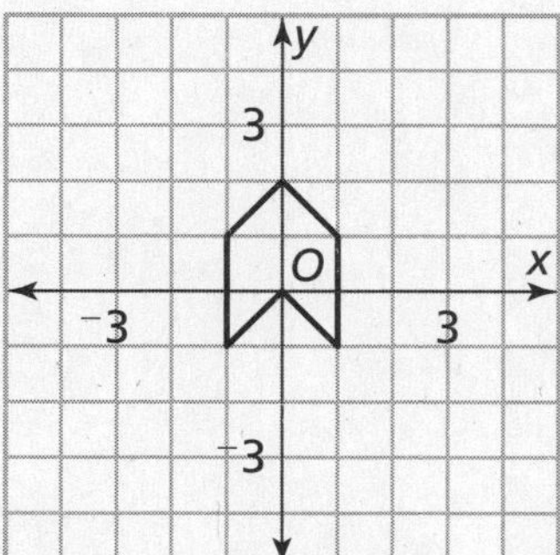

b. Draw the shape in its location after the following sequence of rolls: 1, 6, 4, What are the new coordinates of a general point (x, y) on the shape after this sequence of rolls?

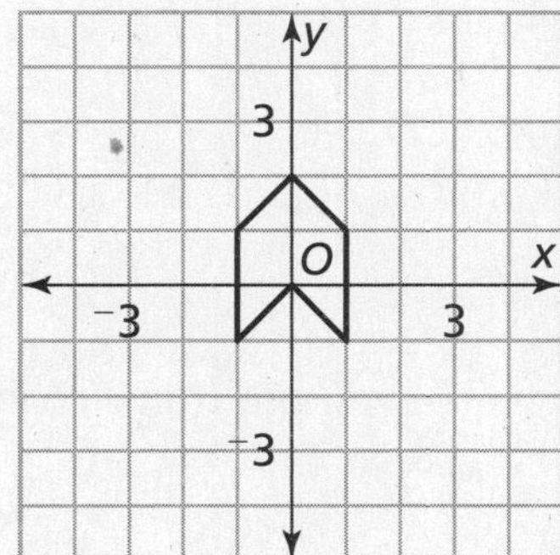

c. What sequence of rolls will produce a final image whose coordinates are all negative?

Additional Practice *(continued)*

19. Describe two different sets of transformations that would move square *PQRS* onto square *WXYZ*.

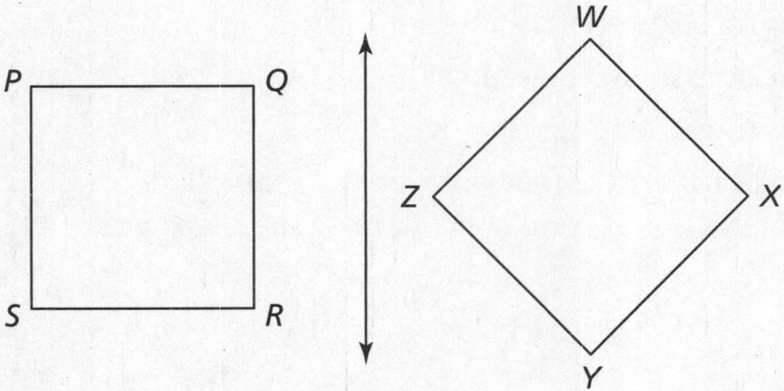

20. Use the figure below to answer (a)–(g).

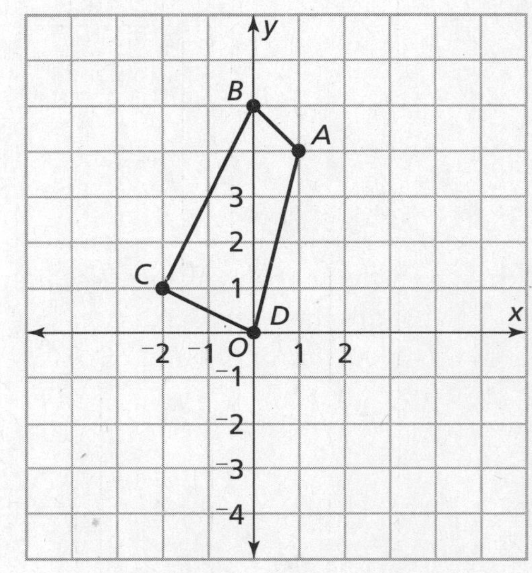

a. Write the coordinates of the points *A*, *B*, *C*, *D*.

b. Write the coordinates of the image of *ABCD* after a reflection in the *x*-axis.

c. Write the coordinates of the image of *ABCD* after a reflection in the *y*-axis.

d. Write the coordinates of the image of *ABCD* after a translation of 3 units to the right.

e. Write the coordinates of the image of *ABCD* after a translation of 4 units to the left.

f. Write the coordinates of the image of *ABCD* after a translation of 2 units up.

g. Write the coordinates of the image of *ABCD* after a translation of 1 unit down.

21. Use the figure below to answer parts (a)–(e).

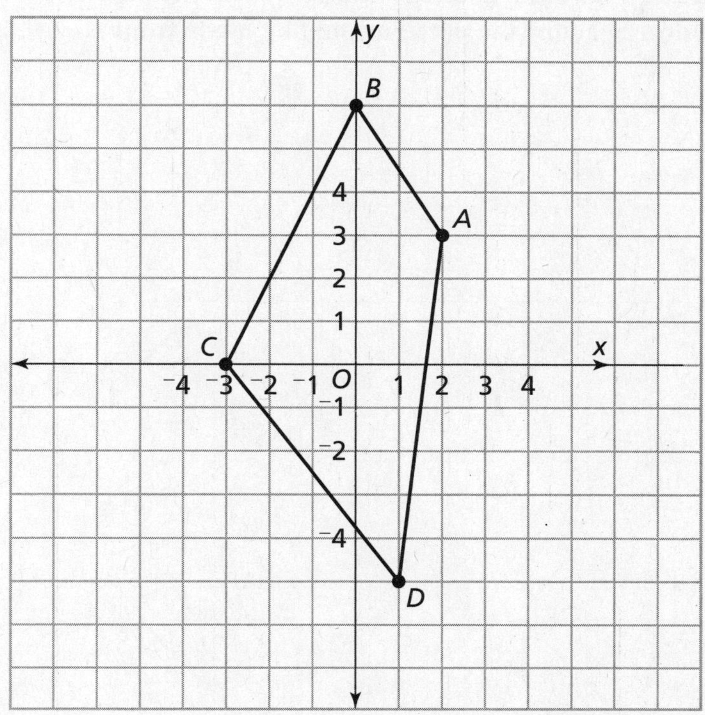

a. Write the coordinates of the points *A, B, C, D*.

b. Write the coordinates of the image of *ABCD* after a reflection in the line $x = 1$.

c. Write the coordinates of the image of *ABCD* after a reflection in the line $x = -2$.

d. Write the coordinates of the image of *ABCD* after a reflection in the line $y = 1$.

e. Write the coordinates of the image of *ABCD* after a reflection in the line $y = -3$.

Name ______________________ Date ____________ Class ____________

Additional Practice (continued)

For Exercises 22 and 23, suppose the pattern in the graph continues in both directions. Identify a basic design element that could be copied and transformed to make the entire pattern, and describe how the pattern could be made from that design element.

22.

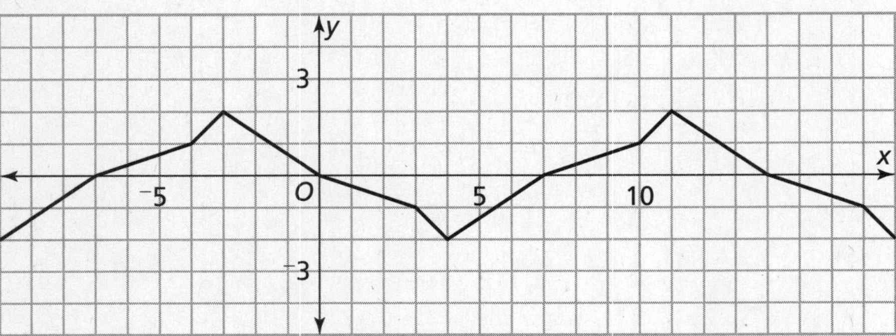

23.

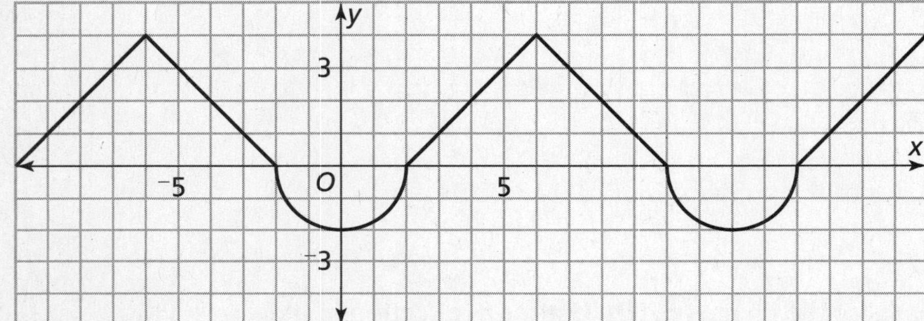

24. Plot the points (2, 4), (3, 5), (5, 5), (4, 4), (5, 3), and (3, 3) on a coordinate grid. Form a polygon by connecting the points in order and then connecting the last point to the first point. Reflect the polygon in the *y*-axis. Then translate the image 6 units to the right. Finally, rotate the second image 90° about the origin. What are the coordinates of the vertices of the final image?

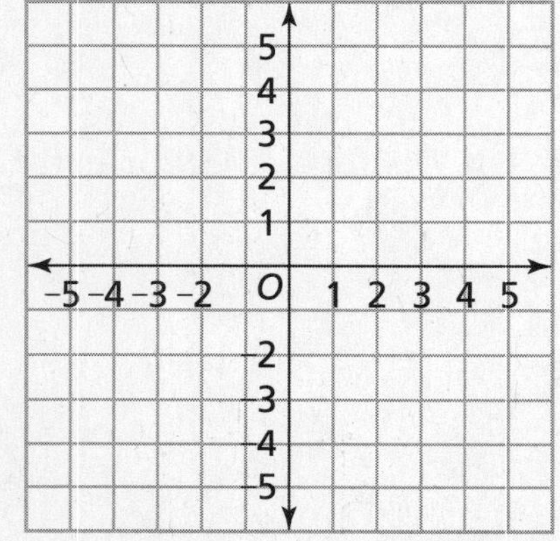

Name ______________________________ Date ____________ Class ____________

Skill: Analyzing Transformations

Investigation 2

Kaleidoscopes, Hubcaps, and Mirrors

Figure II is the image of Figure I. Identify the transformation as a translation, a reflection, or a rotation.

1. 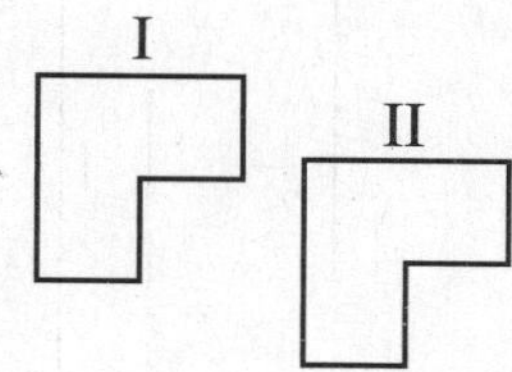

2. 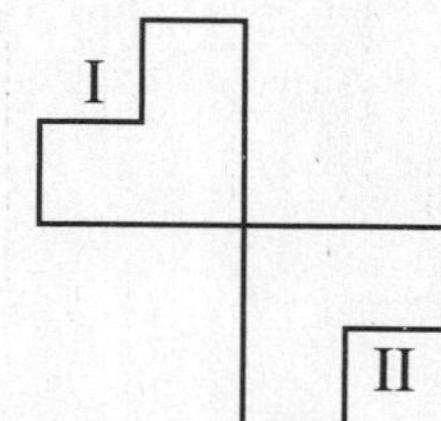

3. 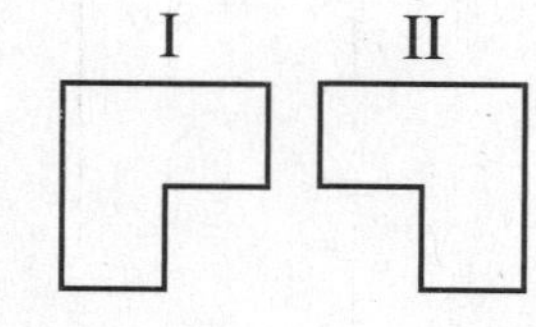

4. 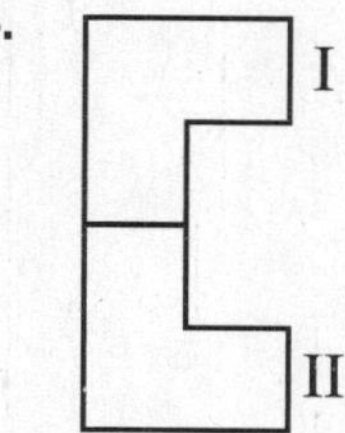

Describe the symmetries of each tessellation. Copy a portion of the tessellation, and draw any centers of rotational symmetry or lines of symmetry.

5. 

6. 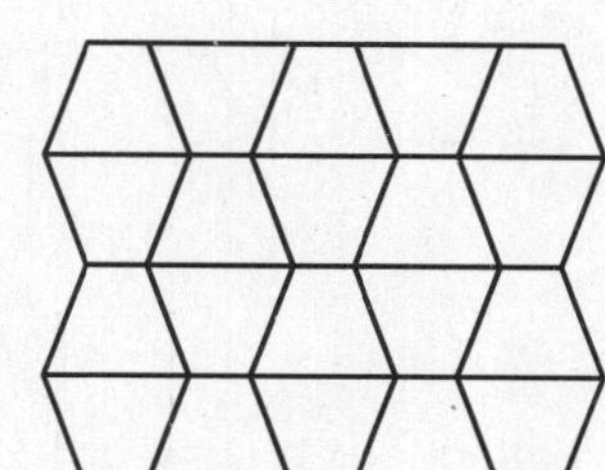

7. 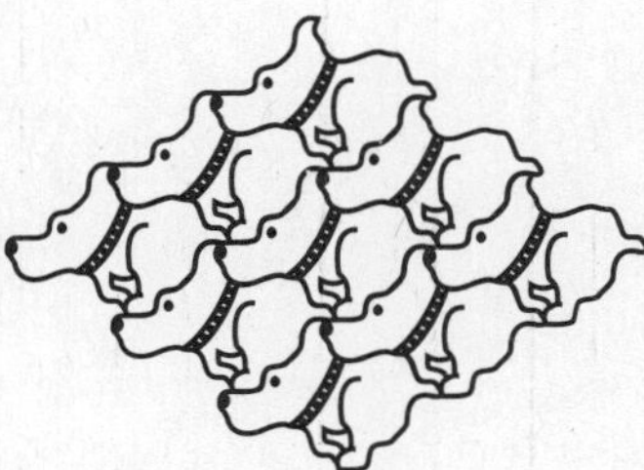

8. 

9. 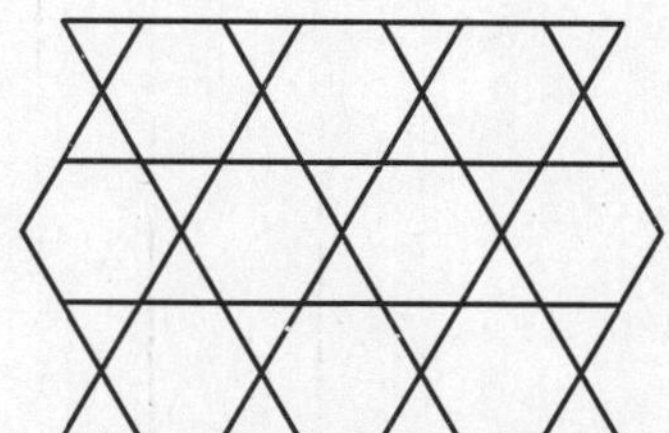

10. 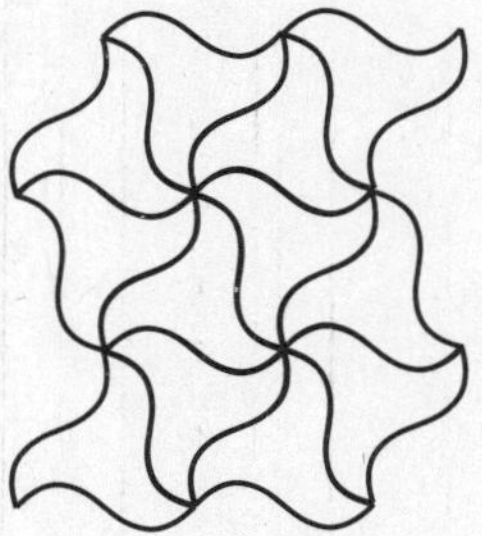

Additional Practice

1. For each pair of triangles, match each of the sides and angles of the first shape with their corresponding congruent part in the second shape.

a.

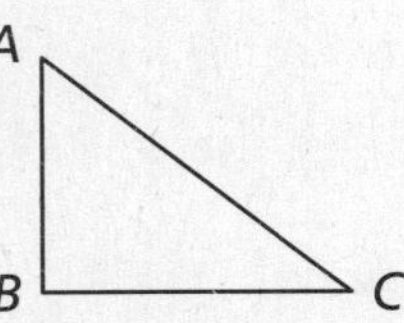

b.

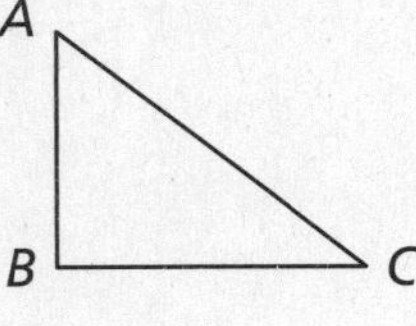

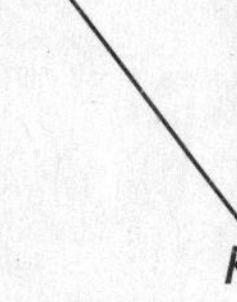

c.

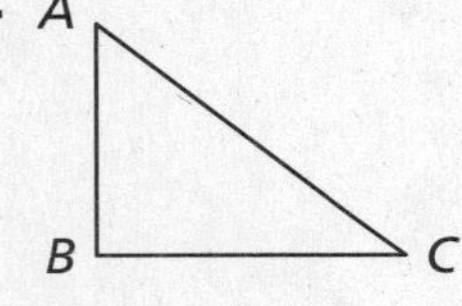

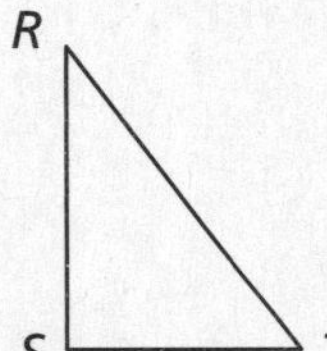

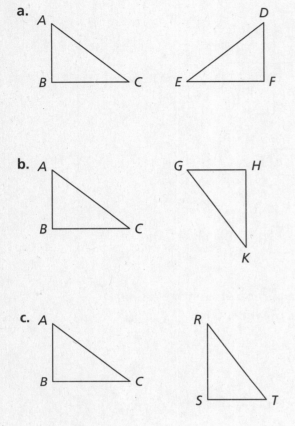

2. For each pair of quadrilaterals, match each of the sides and angles of the first shape with their corresponding congruent parts in the second shape.

a.

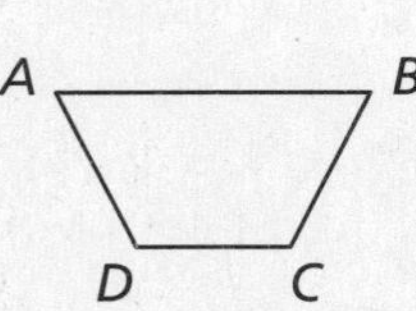

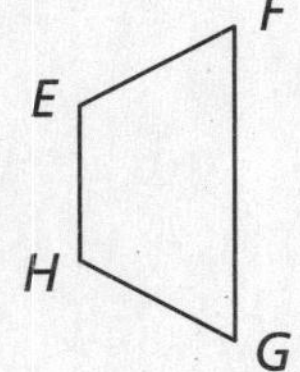

b.

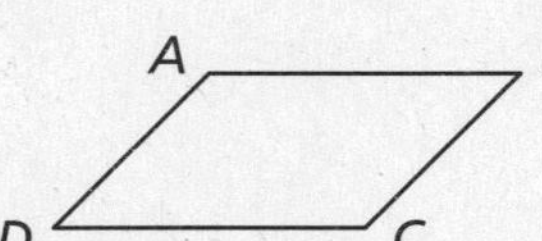

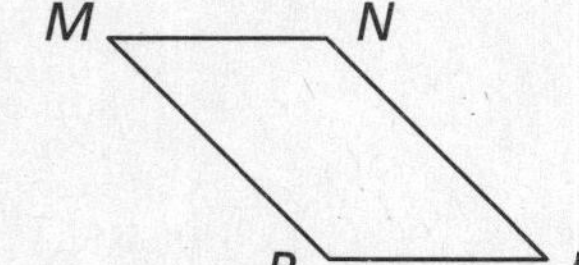

Additional Practice *(continued)*

3. Use the figure of square *JKLM* below to answer (a) and (b).

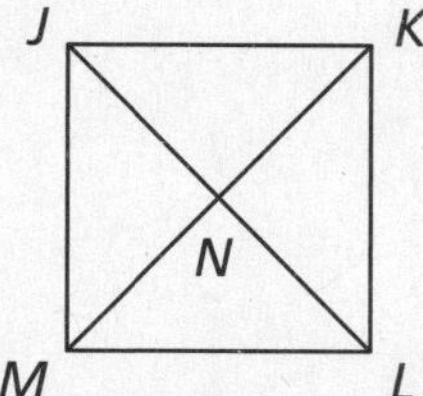

a. List all triangles in the figure above which are congruent to triangle *JNM*. Explain.

b. List all triangles congruent to triangle *MKL*. Explain.

4. The figure below is a parallelogram. Complete the chart.

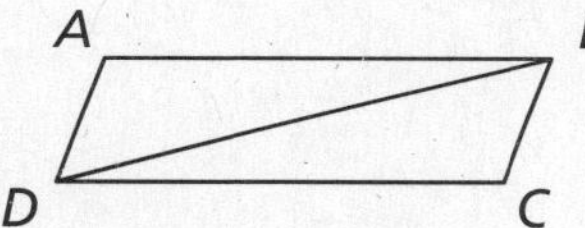

Sets of Congruent Triangles	Evidence for Congruence

5. The figure below is a parallelogram. Complete the chart.

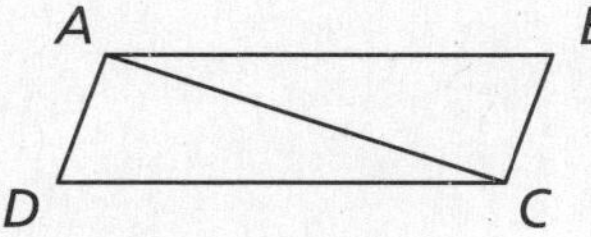

Sets of Congruent Triangles	Evidence for Congruence

6. The figure below is a parallelogram. Complete the chart.

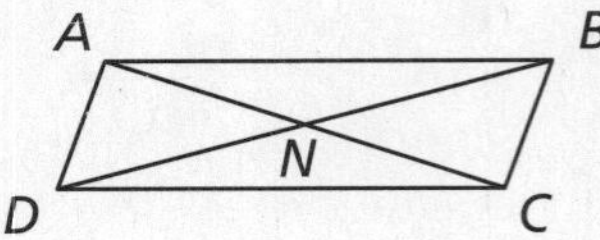

Sets of Congruent Triangles	Evidence for Congruence

7. Rotate triangle ABC below 90º counterclockwise about point A.

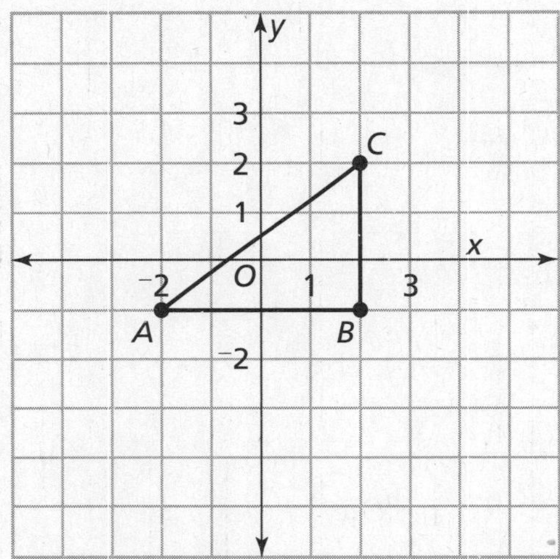

a. Write the coordinates for points A, B and C.

b. Write the coordinates for the images of points A, B and C after the rotation.

c. Is the image of the triangle ABC congruent to triangle ABC? Explain your reasoning.

Name ______________________________ Date ____________ Class ____________

Additional Practice

Investigation 4

1. The figure below is a kite.

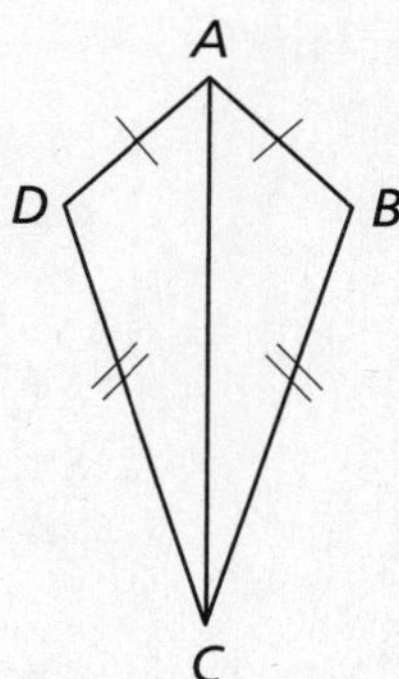

a. Are triangles *ABC* and *ADC* congruent? Explain.

b. Does $\overline{AC}$ bisect angle *DAB*? Explain.

c. Does $\overline{AC}$ bisect angle *DCB*?

2. Triangle *ABC* below is isosceles.

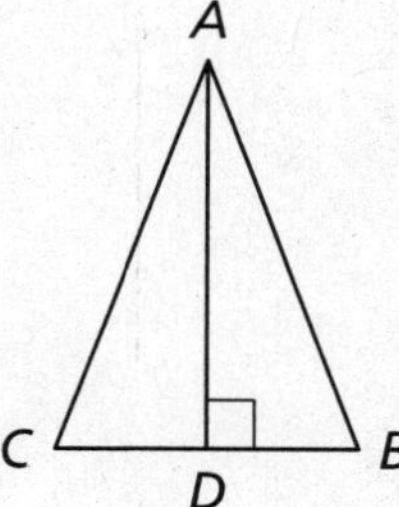

a. Are triangles *ADB* and *ADC* congruent? Explain.

b. Does $\overline{AD}$ bisect angle *CAB*? Explain.

Additional Practice *(continued)*

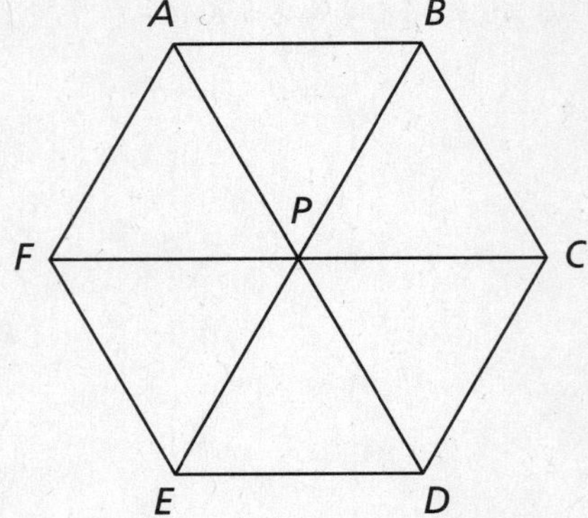

3. Figure $ABCDEF$ at the right is a regular hexagon with 60º rotation symmetry about point P.

a. What line segments are congruent to $\overline{AP}$? Explain.

b. What angles are congruent to angle PAB? Explain.

4. Information about triangle ABC is given below. Determine whether you can draw a congruent copy of triangle ABC given the set of measurements. Explain your reasoning.

a. $\overline{AB} = 5$ cm, $\overline{BC} = 7$ cm, $\angle B = 40°$

b. $\overline{AB} = 7$cm, $\overline{AC} = 5$ cm, $\angle B = 40°$

c. $\overline{AB} = 5$ cm, $\angle A = 50°$, $\angle B = 40°$

d. $\overline{AB} = 5$ cm, $\angle B = 40°$, $\angle C = 90°$

e. $\overline{AB} = 5$ cm, $\overline{BC} = 7$ cm, $\overline{CA} = 6$ cm

f. $\angle A = 50°$, $\angle B = 40°$, $\angle C = 90°$

Name ______________________ Date ___________ Class ___________

Skill: Using Congruence

Complete each congruence statement.

1. 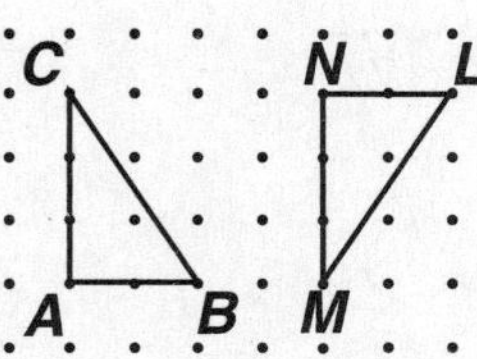

$\Delta ABC \cong$

2. 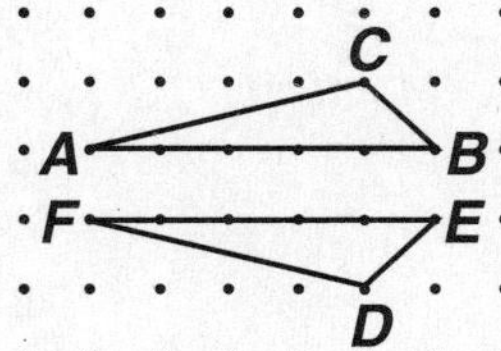

$\Delta ABC \cong$

3. 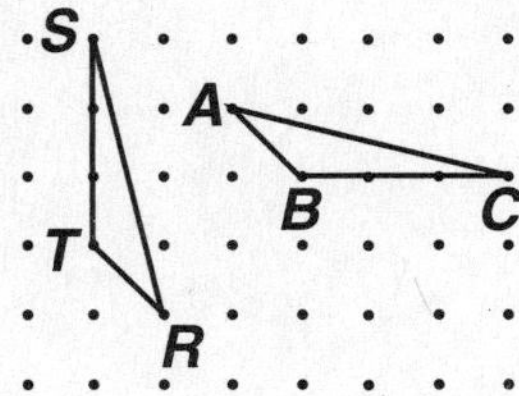

$\Delta ABC \cong$

For Exercises 4–5, use the diagram at the right.

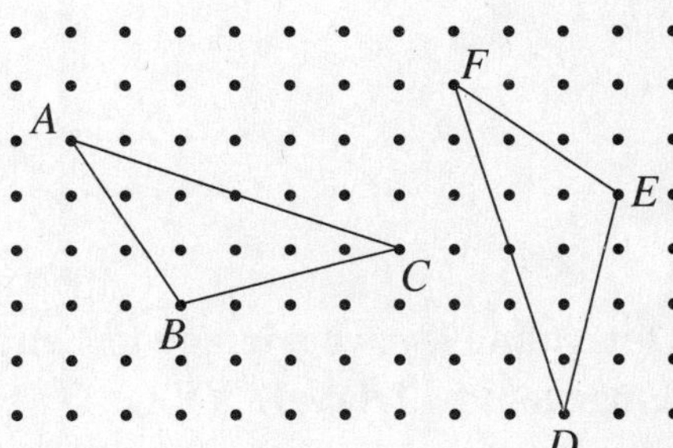

4. a. $\angle ABC \cong$

   b. $\overline{AB} \cong$

   c. $\angle F \cong$

5. a. $\Delta ABC \cong$

   b. $\Delta BAC \cong$

   c. $\Delta CAB \cong$

Name ______________________ Date __________ Class __________

Skill: Using Congruence *(continued)*

Determine whether each pair of triangles is congruent. Explain.

6.

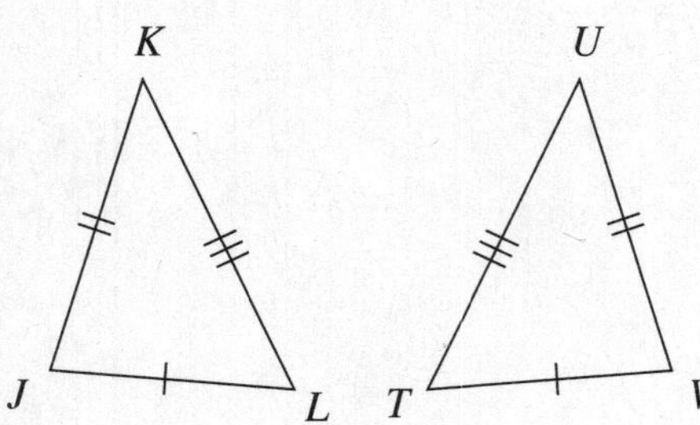

7.

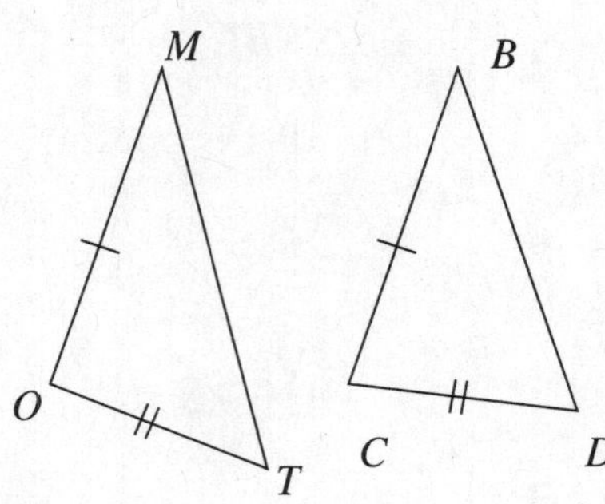

8.

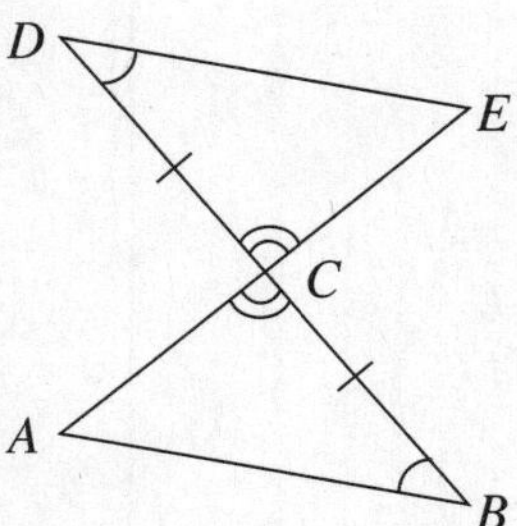

9.

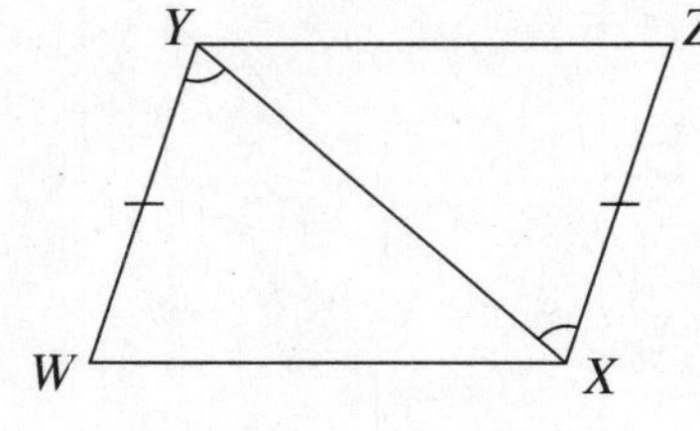

Determine if each triangle has enough information to say for certain they are congruent to Triangle *XYZ*.

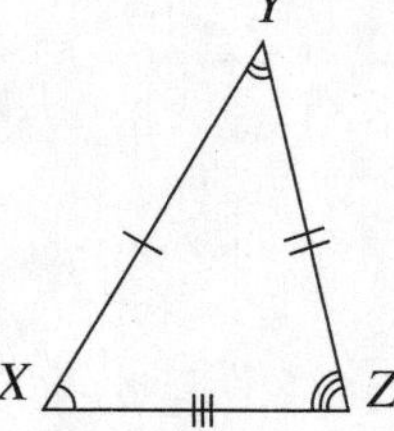

10.

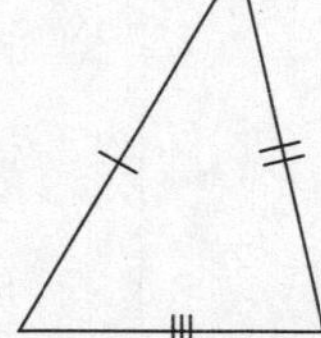

11.

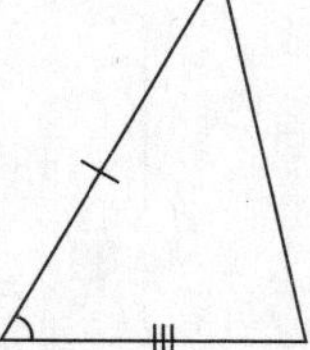

12.

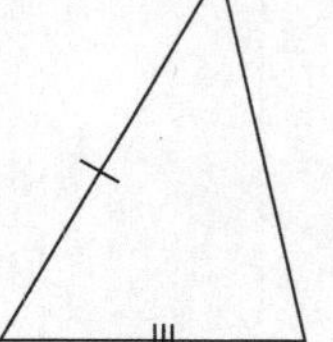

Name ______________________________ Date ____________ Class ____________

Additional Practice

Investigation 5

Kaleidoscopes, Hubcaps, and Mirrors

For Exercises 1–6, refer to the grid below.

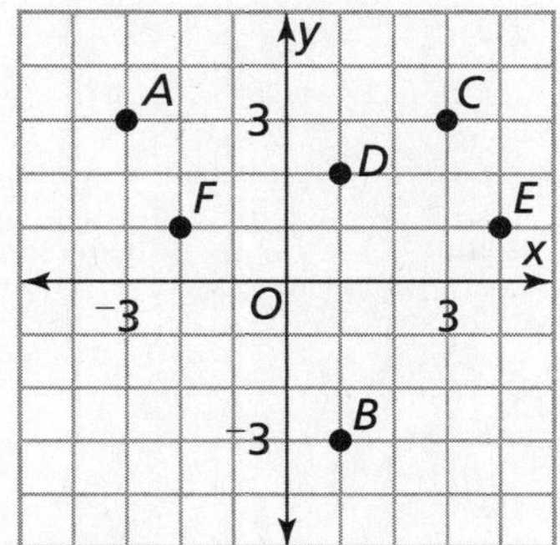

1. What are the coordinates of the image of point A under a translation that moves point $(1, 2)$ onto point $(-2, 0)$?

2. What are the coordinates of the image of point B under a translation that moves point $(1, 2)$ onto point $(4, -4)$?

3. What are the coordinates of the image of point C under a translation that moves point $(1, 2)$ onto point $(-3, -2)$?

4. What are the coordinates of the image of point D under a reflection in the x-axis?

5. What are the coordinates of the image of point E under a reflection in the y-axis?

6. What are the coordinates of the image of point F under a reflection in the line $y = x$?

7. Identify two congruent shapes in the figure below, and explain how you could use symmetry transformations to move one shape onto the other.

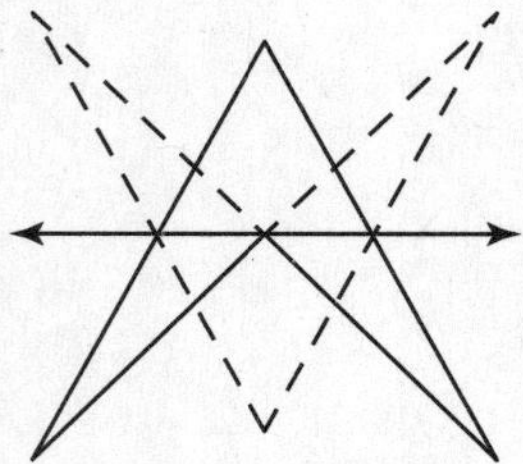

For Exercises 8–9, refer to the grid below.

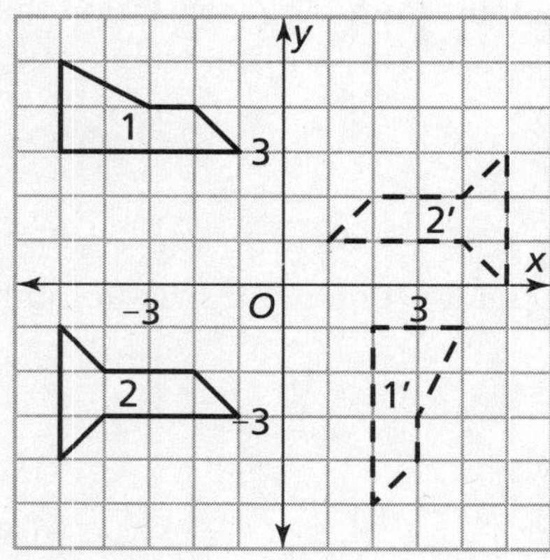

8. Describe how you could move Shape 1 to exactly match Shape 1′ by using at least one translation and at least one reflection.

9. Describe how you could move Shape 2 to exactly match Shape 2′ by using at least one translation and at least one reflection.

Additional Practice *(continued)*

For Exercises 10–12, refer to the grid below.

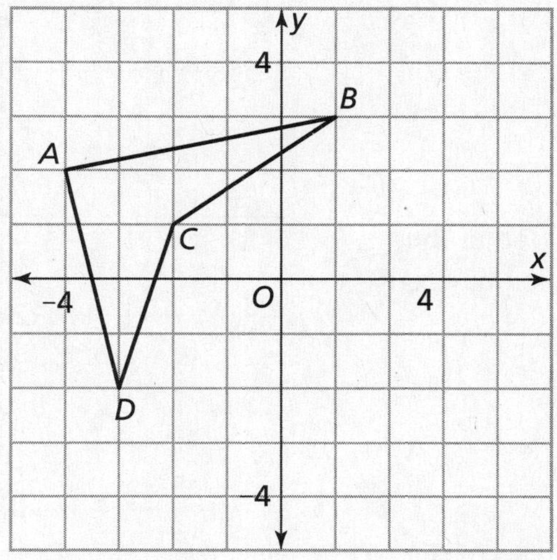

10. a. On the above grid, draw the final image created by rotating polygon *ABCD* 90° counterclockwise about the origin and then reflecting the image in the *x*-axis.

b. On the above grid, draw the final image created by reflecting polygon *ABCD* in the *x*-axis and then rotating the image 90° counterclockwise about the origin.

c. Are the final images in parts (a) and (b) the same? Explain.

11. What single transformation is equivalent to a counterclockwise rotation of 90° about the origin followed by a rotation of 270° counterclockwise about the origin?

12. What single transformation is equivalent to a reflection in the *y*-axis, followed by a reflection in the *y*-axis, followed by a reflection in the *y*-axis?

Additional Practice *(continued)*

13. Use the figure at the right to answer parts (a)–(c).

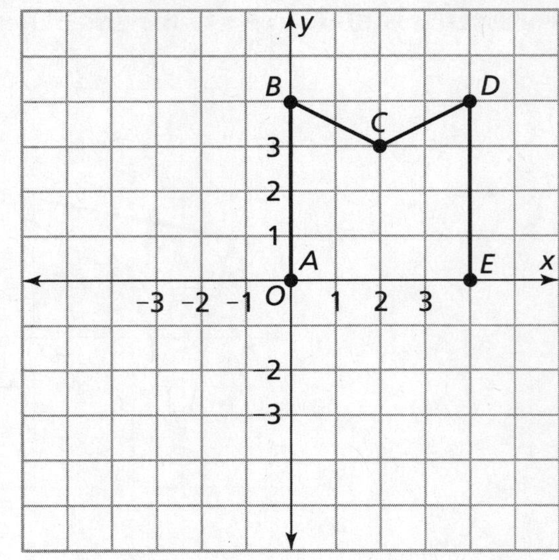

a. Write the coordinates for point *A*, *B*, *C*, *D*, *E*.

b. If the figure (the "M") was reflected in the *x*-axis, write the coordinates of the images of *A*, *B*, *C*, *D* and *E*.

c. If the figure (the "M") was reflected in the *y*-axis, write the coordinates of the images of *A*, *B*, *C*, *D* and *E*.

14. Use the figure at the right to answer parts (a)–(c).

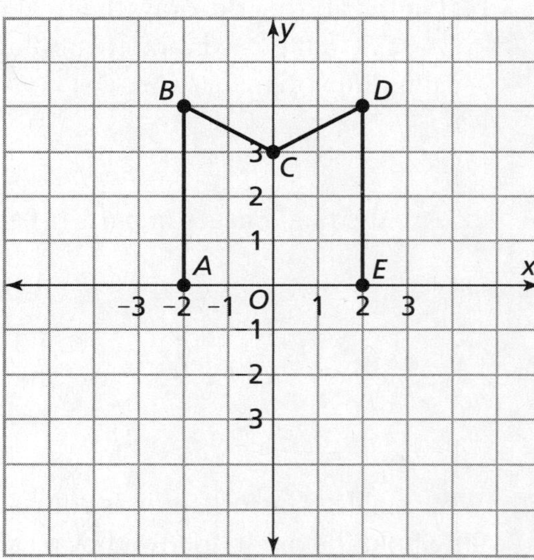

a. Write the coordinates for point *A*, *B*, *C*, *D*, *E*.

b. If the figure (the "M") was reflected in the *x*-axis, write the coordinates of the images of *A*, *B*, *C*, *D* and *E*.

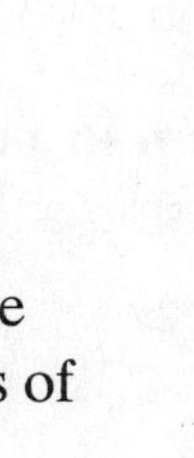

c. If the figure (the "M") was reflected in the *y*-axis, write the coordinates of the images of *A*, *B*, *C*, *D* and *E*.

Name _______________ Date ___________ Class ___________

Additional Practice *(continued)*

15. Use the figure at the right to answer parts (a)–(c).

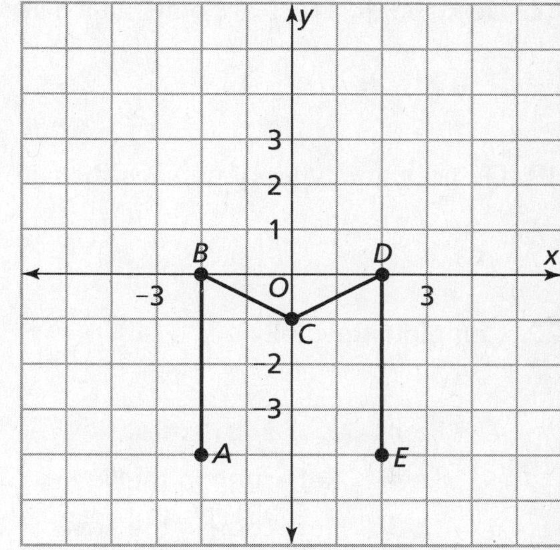

a. Write the coordinates for point A, B, C, D, E.

b. If the figure (the "M") was reflected in the x-axis, write the coordinates of the images of A, B, C, D and E.

c. If the figure (the "M") was reflected in the y-axis, write the coordinates of the images of A, B, C, D and E.

16. Complete the table:

Point	Transformation	Coordinates of the Image
(3, 2)	Reflection in the *x*-axis	
(3, 1)	Reflection in the *x*-axis	
(3, 0)	Reflection in the *x*-axis	
(3, −1)	Reflection in the *x*-axis	
(3, −2)	Reflection in the *x*-axis	

17. Complete the table:

Point	Transformation	Coordinates of the Image
(3, 2)	Reflection in the *y*-axis	
(2, 2)	Reflection in the *y*-axis	
(1, 2)	Reflection in the *y*-axis	
(0, 2)	Reflection in the *y*-axis	
(−1, 2)	Reflection in the *y*-axis	

Additional Practice *(continued)*

18. Describe the types of points, which are fixed after a reflection in the x-axis.

19. Describe the types of points, which are fixed after a reflection in the y-axis.

20. Complete the table:

Point	Transformation	Coordinates of the Image
(2, 4)	Reflection in the line $y = x$	
(2, 3)	Reflection in the line $y = x$	
(2, 2)	Reflection in the line $y = x$	
(2, 1)	Reflection in the line $y = x$	
(2, 0)	Reflection in the line $y = x$	

21. Complete the table:

Point	Transformation	Coordinates of the Image
(2, 4)	Reflection in the line $y = x$	
(3, −4)	Reflection in the line $y = x$	
(4, 4)	Reflection in the line $y = x$	
(−5, 4)	Reflection in the line $y = x$	
(−2, 0)	Reflection in the line $y = x$	

22. Describe the types of points, which are fixed after a reflection in the line $y = x$.

Skill: Transforming Coordinates

$\Delta A'B'C'$ is a reflection of ΔABC over the x-axis. Draw $\Delta A'B'C'$ and complete each statement.

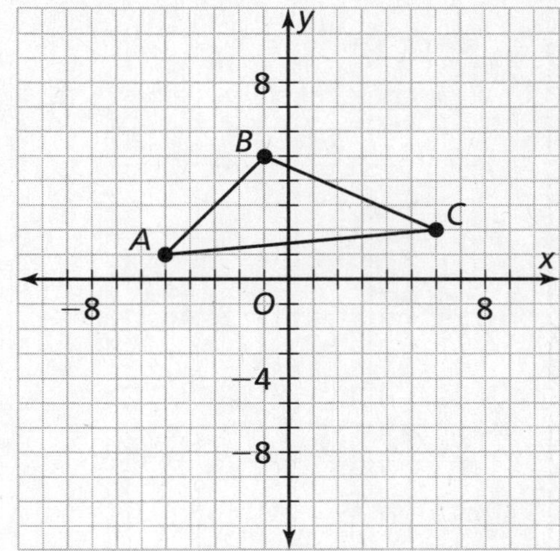

1. $A(-5, 1) \rightarrow A'(x, y)$

2. $B(-1, 5) \rightarrow B'(x, y)$

3. $C(6, 2) \rightarrow C'(x, y)$

Graph each point and its reflection across the indicated axis. Write the coordinates of the reflected point.

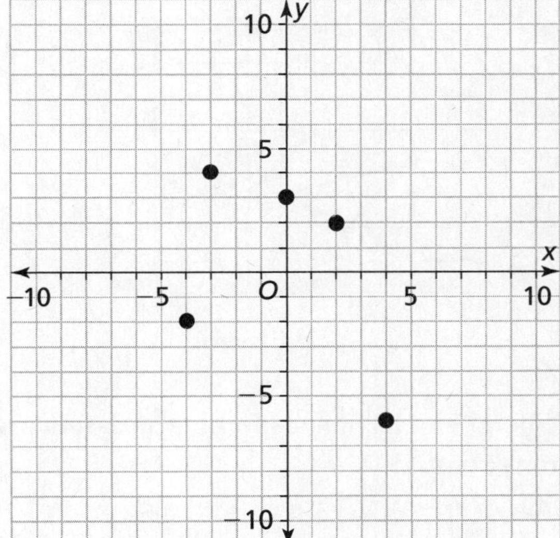

4. $(-3, 4)$ across the y-axis

5. $(-4, -2)$ across the x-axis

6. $(2, 2)$ across the x-axis

7. $(0, 3)$ across the x-axis

8. $(4, -6)$ across the y-axis

9. $(-4, -2)$ across the y-axis

Name ________________________ Date ____________ Class ____________

Skill: Transforming Coordinates *(continued)*

Write a rule to describe each translation.

10. $(x, y) \rightarrow$

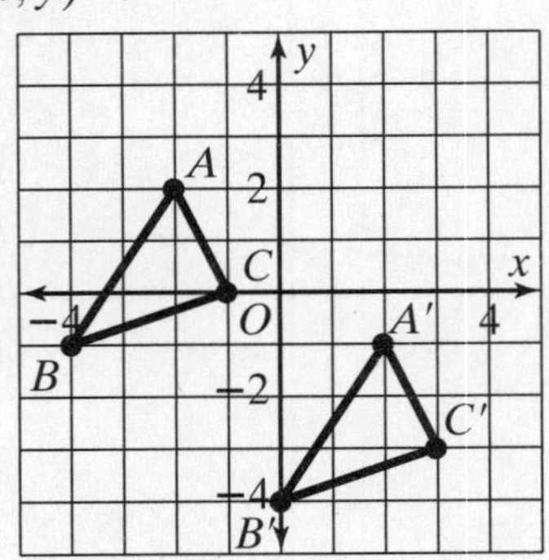

11. $(x, y) \rightarrow$

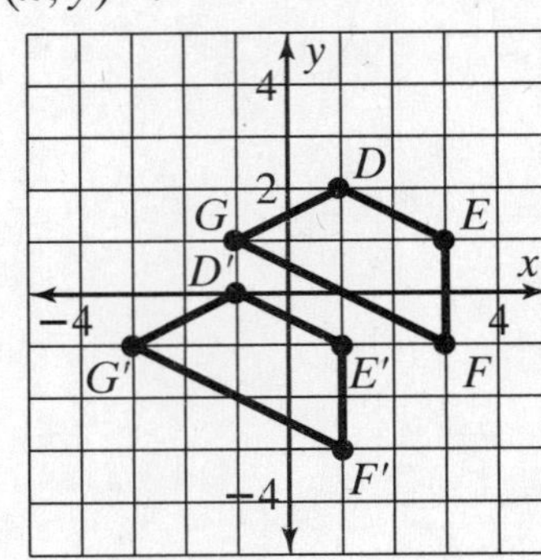

12. $(x, y) \rightarrow$

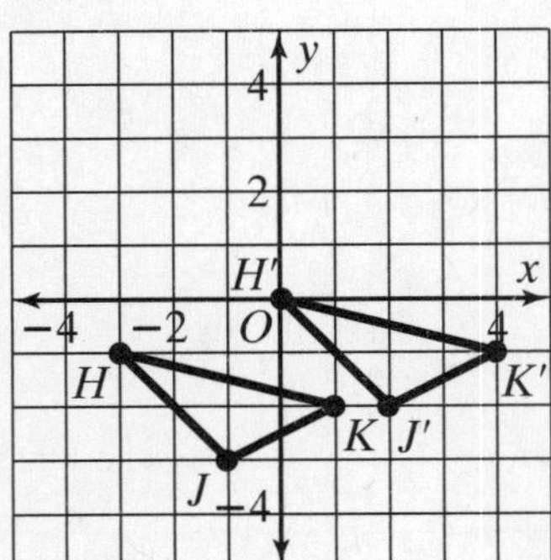

13. $(x, y) \rightarrow$

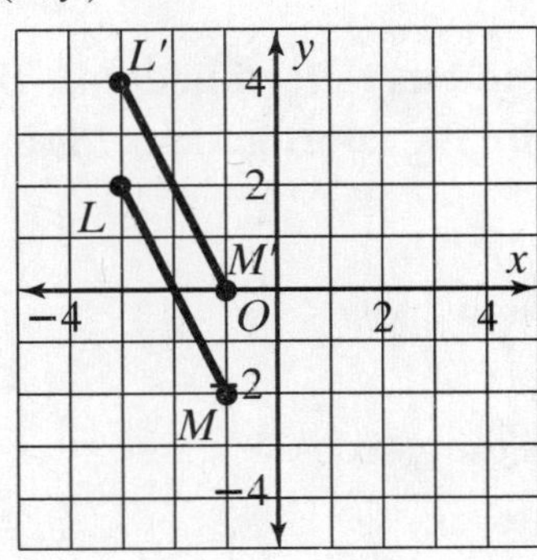

A point and its image after a translation are given. Write a rule to describe the translation.

14. $A(9, -4), A'(2, -1)$ $(x, y)\rightarrow$

15. $B(-3, 5), B'(-5, -3)$ $(x, y)\rightarrow$

Write a rule to describe each statement.

16. In a 90° rotation, move point (x, y) to

17. In a 180° rotation, move point (x, y) to

Name ______________________ Date ____________ Class ____________

Additional Practice

Investigation 1

Say It With Symbols

The rectangle below has length ℓ and width w.

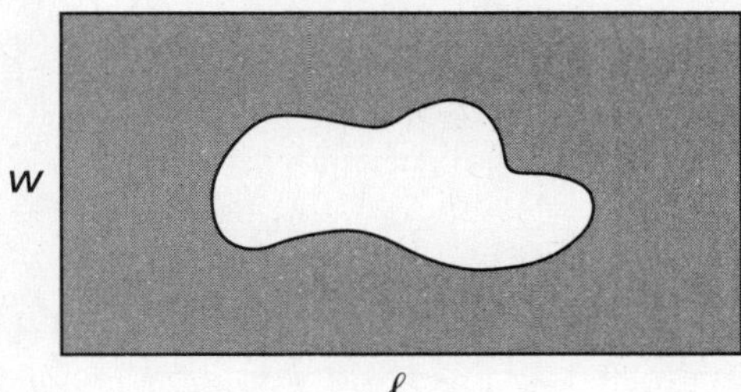

1. Write two equations for the perimeter p of the rectangle.

2. Suppose the length of the rectangle is equal to twice the width, or $2w$.
   a. If the width of the rectangle is 1.5, what is the length?
   b. If the width is 2, what is the perimeter?
   c. Write two equations for the perimeter of the rectangle p in terms of only the width w.

3. Suppose $\ell = 14$ meters and $w = 6.5$ meters, and the area of the blob is 38 square meters. What is the area of the shaded region inside the rectangle? Show how you found your answer.

4. Write an equation for the area A of the shaded region inside the rectangle if the area of the blob is Q square meters.

For Exercises 5–8, write two expressions that are equivalent to the given expression.

5. $7(x - 4)$

6. $x(5 - 6) + 13x - 10$

7. $2.5(8 - 2x) + 5(x + 1)$

8. $3(x + 10) - 3(2 - 4x)$

Additional Practice (continued)

9. a. Complete the table below.

	Value of the expression when...				
Expression	$x = 1$	$x = 2$	$x = 5$	$x = 6.5$	$x = 27$
$3x + 6$					
$3(x + 2)$					
$3(x + 1) + 3$					

b. What patterns do you notice?

c. Are these expressions related?

d. How might you verify your answer to part (c)?

For Exercises 10–12 complete parts (a)–(c).

a. For each expression, write an equation of the form $y =$ *expression*. Make a table and a graph of the two equations. Show x values from -5 to 5 on the graph.

b. Based on your table and graph, tell whether you think the two expressions are equivalent.

c. Use the properties you have learned to verify their equivalence or explain why you think they are not equivalent.

10. $4(x + 2)$ and $4x + 8$

11. $4(x + 2)$ and $4x + 4$

12. $3 - 6x$ and $3(1 - 2x)$

13. For each pair of expressions, show that they are equivalent by drawing a rectangle divided into four sections. Label the sections to support your argument.

    a. 32×47 and $1{,}200 + 80 + 210 + 14$

    b. 3.2×4.7 and $12 + 0.8 + 2.1 + 0.14$

    c. $(3 + x)(4 + y)$ and $12 + 4x + 3y + xy$

14. All the expressions below contain the same string of symbols. Only the placement of the parentheses varies. Which, if any, of the expressions are equivalent?

    a. $6 + 3x + 8 - 4x + 4$

    b. $6 + 3(x + 8) - 4x + 4$

    c. $(6 + 3x) + 8 - 4x + 4$

    d. $6 + 3x + 8 - 4(x + 4)$

15. Use the distributive and commutative properties to determine whether the following statements are equal for all values of x.

a. $3(x + 1) + x$ and $4x + 1$

b. $6x$ and $(12x - 4x) - 2x$

c. $6x$ and $12x - (4x - 2x)$

d. $7x + 5x + 1$ and $12x + 1$

16. Dave made the following sketch, which includes four right isosceles triangles and four trapezoids for the number of tiles around the pool in Problem 1.1.

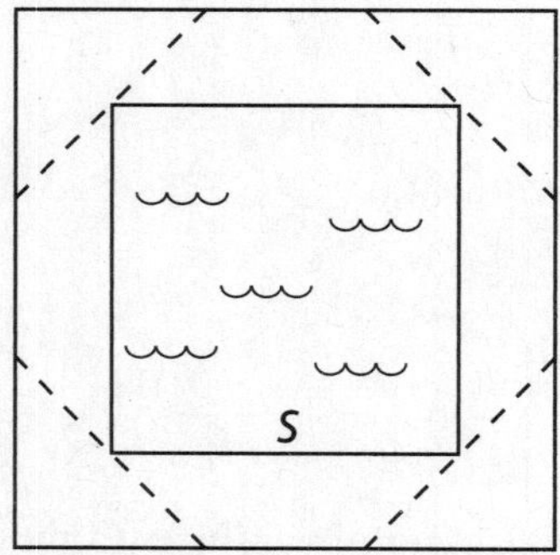

a. Write an equation relating the number of tiles N to the length of the side s that Dave might have used to represent his sketch and his thinking about the Tiling Pools problem.

b. Check to see if your equation is equivalent to those found in Problem 1.1.

Name ______________________ Date __________ Class __________

Skill: Writing Equivalent Expressions

Use the Distributive Property to write each expression in expanded form.

1. $2(x + 6)$

2. $-5(8 - b)$

3. $4(-x + 7)$

4. $-\frac{3}{4}(12 - 16d)$

5. $\frac{2}{3}(6h - 1)$

6. $(-3.2x + 2.1)(-6)$

7. $3.5(3x - 8)$

8. $4(x + 7)$

9. $-2.5(2a - 4)$

10. $\frac{2}{3}(12 - 15d)$

11. $-2(k - 11)$

12. $-\frac{1}{3}(6h + 15)$

Skill: Writing Equivalent Expressions *(continued)*

Use the Distributive Property to write each expression in factored form.

13. $4v - 7 + 8v + 4 - 5$

14. $5(g + 8) + 7 + 4g$

15. $12h - 17 - h + 16 - 2h$

16. $7(e - 8) + 12 - 2e$

17. $-3y + 7 + y + 6y$

18. $(3.2m + 1.8) - 1.07m$

Write each expression in expanded form.

19. $(x - 4)(x - 6)$

20. $(m - 15)(m - 20)$

21. $(y - 7)(y - 6)$

22. $(x - 9)(x - 5)$

Insert parentheses on the left side to make each number sentence true.

23. $3 + 5 \cdot 8 = 64$

24. $4 \cdot 6 - 2 + 7 = 23$

25. $10 \div 3 + 2 \cdot 4 = 8$

26. $3 + 6 \cdot 2 = 18$

Name ______________________ Date ____________ Class ____________

Skill: Operations With Rational Numbers

Write each expression as a single number.

1. $\frac{1}{4} + \left(-\frac{3}{4}\right)$

2. $\frac{2}{3} + \left(-\frac{1}{3}\right)$

3. $-\frac{7}{12} + \frac{1}{6}$

4. $2\frac{2}{3} + (-1)$

5. $-3\frac{3}{4} + 1\frac{1}{2}$

6. $2\frac{1}{3} + \left(-4\frac{2}{3}\right)$

7. $18.3 - (-8.1)$

8. $-3 - (-15)$

9. $6.4 - 17$

10. $\frac{3}{4} - 1\frac{1}{4}$

11. $-\frac{1}{3} - \frac{2}{3}$

12. $-\frac{1}{4} - \left(-\frac{3}{4}\right)$

Name ________________________________ Date __________ Class __________

Skill: Operations With Rational Numbers *(continued)*

13. $(-2)(8)$

14. $(-6)(-9)$

15. $(-3)^4$

16. -2^5

17. $(6)(-8)$

18. $(-14)^2$

19. $2(-4)(-6)$

20. $-30 \div (-5)$

21. $\frac{-52}{-13}$

22. $(-8)(5)(-3)$

23. -7^2

24. -3^5

25. $\frac{-68}{17}$

26. $\frac{(-4)(-13)}{-26}$

27. $\frac{225}{(-3)(-5)}$

28. $2^4 - 3^2 + 5^2$

29. $(-8)^2 - 4^3$

30. $32 \div (-7 + 5)^3$

31. $\frac{3}{4} \div \left(-\frac{3}{7}\right)$

32. $18 + 4^2 \div (-8)$

33. $26 \div [4-(-9)]$

Name ______________________ Date __________ Class __________

Additional Practice

For Exercises 1–26, evaluate the expression for the given value of x.

1. $3.5x - 10$ when $x = 2$
2. $45 - 2x$ when $x = 6$
3. $-3 - x$ when $x = \frac{1}{2}$
4. $4x + 9$ when $x = 11$
5. $2x^2$ when $x = 8$
6. $11 - 3x^2$ when $x = 1$
7. $4.5 + x^2$ when $x = 1.5$
8. $6x^2 + 13$ when $x = -10$
9. $6x^2 + x - 11$ when $x = 2$
10. $6x^2 + x - 11$ when $x = -2$
11. $12 - 2x^2 + 5x$ when $x = -4$
12. $12 - 2x^2 + 5x$ when $x = 4$
13. $x(31 - x)$ when $x = 3$
14. $(x + 5)(x - 1)$ when $x = 0$
15. $(x - 1.5)(x + 42)$ when $x = 1.5$
16. $(31 - x)x$ when $x = -3$
17. $\frac{36}{x^2}$ when $x = -6$
18. $\frac{x^2}{24}(x + 7)$ when $x = -7$
19. $42(x + 1)$ when $x = 4$
20. $\frac{3(16 - x)}{2x}$ when $x = 10$
21. $\frac{x}{4} + 6(x - 12)$ when $x = 12$
22. $7x(3 + x)$ when $x = -4$
23. $7x^2 - x + 10$ when $x = 2$
24. $8x - 2x(6 - x)$ when $x = 0$
25. $0.5x^2 + x - 20$ when $x = 10$
26. $(x + 7)(x - 2)$ when $x = -5$

Additional Practice *(continued)*

27. The Metropolis Middle School volleyball team is operating the concession stand at school basketball games to help raise money for new uniforms. The profit in dollars P from operating the stand is given by the equation $P = N - 0.5\left(\frac{N}{5} + 300\right)$, where N is the total number of items sold.

a. How much money will the volleyball team raise if they sell 400 items?

b. How much money will the volleyball team raise if they sell 550 items?

c. If the team needs to raise $1,000 for new uniforms, will they have to sell more than or fewer than 1,000 items? Explain your reasoning.

d. Write an equivalent equation for P.

28. Each side of the figure at the right has length x.

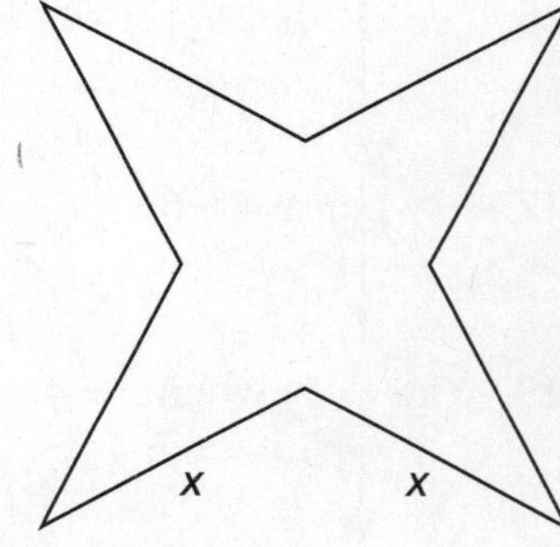

a. If $x = 3.5$, what is the perimeter of the figure?

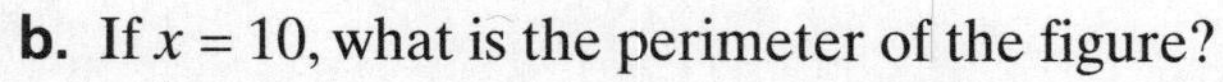

b. If $x = 10$, what is the perimeter of the figure?

c. Write three equivalent expressions for the perimeter P of the figure.

d. Show that your three expressions for the perimeter are equivalent.

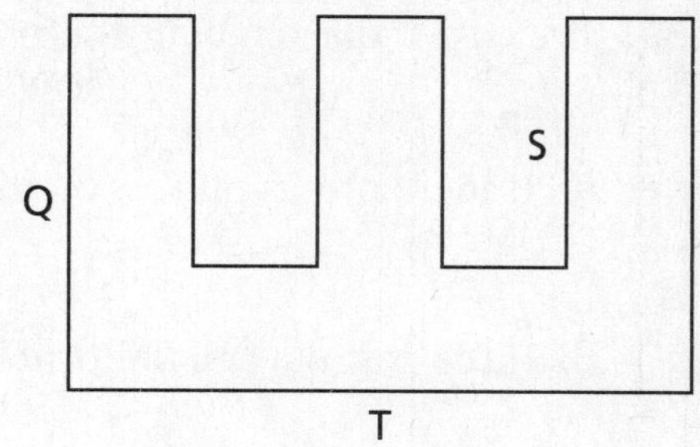

29. Refer to the figure at the right to answer parts (a)–(d).

a. If $Q = 4$ meters, $S = 3$ meters, and $T = 7$ meters, what is the perimeter of the figure?

b. If $Q = 3$ meters, $S = 2.5$ meters, and $T = 4$ meters, what is the perimeter of the figure?

c. Using the variables Q, S, and T, write three equations for the perimeter P of the figure.

d. Using the values from part (a), find the perimeter of the figure using each of your equations. Check or revise your equations if you do not get the same perimeter in each case.

e. Show that your three expressions for the perimeter are equivalent.

30. At Metropolis Middle School, the number of cans N collected for recycling after a basketball game depends on the number of people P who attend the game. The approximate relationship is given by $N = 2.5(P - 40) - 100$.

a. Is the relationship between the number of cans collected and the number of people attending linear or quadratic? Explain.

b. If 400 people attended the game for the semifinals of the district championship, how many cans would you expect to be collected?

c. If 300 cans were collected at a game, how many people would you expect to have attended the game?

d. If 675 cans were collected at another game, how many people would you expect to have attended that game?

31. The cost C of each uniform for the players on an N-person basketball team is given by the equation $C = \frac{(40N + 260)}{N}$.

a. If there are 25 players on the team, what is the cost of each uniform?

b. If the cost of each uniform is $53, how many players are on the team?

c. If the cost of each uniform is $56.25, how many players are on the team?

32. A television video-game company has the following total expenses E and total incomes I for producing x number of videos.

$E = 200 + 11x$ $\qquad$ $I = 120 + x^2$

a. Write an equation to represent the profit P for selling x videos.

b. How many videos must be sold to "break even?"

c. How many videos must be sold to make a profit of $100?

d. Describe how you could use a graph or table to solve parts (b) and (c).

For Exercises 33–44, tell whether the expressions are equivalent, and explain your reasoning.

33. $3x + 5x$ and $8x$

34. $3x + 5$ and $8x$

35. $4(x + 7)$ and $4x + 7$

36. $5(x + 2)$ and $5x + 10$

37. $12 + 8x$ and $4(3 + 2x)$

38. $4x + x + 2x$ and $8x$

39. $7 + 5x$ and $5x + 7$

40. $3x + 8$ and $8x + 3$

41. $5x + 3x + 4x$ and $4x + 5x + 3x$

42. $6 + 2t$ and $2(t + 3)$

43. $2(L + 2) + 2W$ and $2L + 2W + 4$

44. $2L + 2W + 4$ and $2(L + W + 2)$

For Exercises 45–46, complete the statement, with a number or an expression that makes the statement true.

45. $x(4 + \square) = 18x$

46. $2(4 + \square) = 8 + 6x$

47. Find y if $x = -50$: $y = 5(x - 150) + 300 - 3x$.

48. Find y when $x = 4$: $y = 3x + 2(8 - 5x)$.

49. Find y when $x = 10$: $y = 8 - 5(x + 2) + 2x$.

50. Thomas performed the calculations for Exercise 49. Are Thomas's calculations correct? Explain your reasoning.

$y = 8 - 5(10 + 2) + 2(10)$

$y = 3(12) + 20$

$y = 36 + 20$

$y = 56$

Evaluate the expression for the given *x*-value, and describe the order in which you performed the operations. Check your answer with a calculator.

51. $\frac{36}{2x}$ when $x = 6$

52. $\frac{3x + 2}{5}$ when $x = 11$

53. $\frac{50x + 10}{x}$ when $x = 2$

Name ____ Date ____________ Class ____________

Skill: Equations; Expressions With Exponents

Solve each equation for the indicated variable.

1. $8z - 7 = 3z - 7 + 5z$

2. $4s - 12 = -5s + 51$

3. $6 - 4d = 16 - 9d$

4. $4g + 7 = 5g - 1 - g$

Find an equivalent expression.

5. $a^1 \cdot a^2$

6. $-z^3 \cdot z^9$

7. $5x^2 \cdot x^6 \cdot x^3$

Simplify each expression.

8. $\frac{7^5}{7^3}$

9. $\frac{b^{12}}{b^4}$

10. $\frac{g^9}{g^{15}}$

Name ______________________ Date ____________ Class ____________

Additional Practice

Investigation 3

Say It With Symbols

1. a. Write 45 as a product of two factors.

   b. Write 45 as a product of three factors.

   c. Write 45 as a product of two factors, such that one factor is the sum of two terms.

   d. Write $45x$ as a product of two factors.

   e. Write $45x$ as the sum of three terms.

   f. Write $45x$ as a product of two factors, such that one factor is the sum of two terms, in at least two ways.

Write the quadratic equation in factored form.

2. $y = 3x + 21x^2$
3. $q = 72r^2 - 24r$
4. $y = 5x^2 + 10x$
5. $a = 16b - 48b^2$
6. $y = 3(x - 1) + (x - 1)$
7. $y = x^2 + 3x + 2$
8. $y = x(x - 10) + x(2x + 5)$
9. $y = 52x^2 - 13$

For Exercises 10–19, solve each equation for *x* and check your answer.

10. $2x + 5 = 11$
11. $9 + 3x = 30$
12. $4x + 19 = 26 - 3x$
13. $x^2 - 2.5x = 0$

Additional Practice *(continued)*

14. $11x - x^2 = 0$

15. $5x^2 - 2x = x^2 - 10x$

16. $3x(x - 5) = 0$

17. $4.5(x + 1) + 2(x + 1) = 0$

18. $4.5x = x - 7$

19. $81x - 9x^2 = 0$

20. Below is a graph of a parabola.

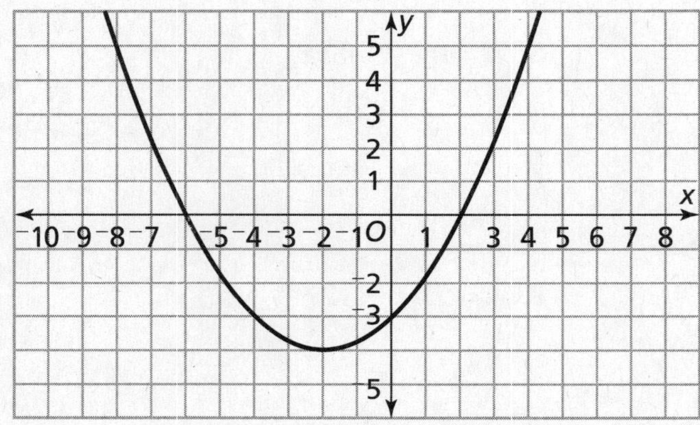

a. What are the coordinates of the maximum or minimum point?

b. What are the coordinates of the x-intercept(s)?

c. What are the coordinates of the y-intercept(s)?

d. Could $y = -(x - 4)^2 + 2$ be the equation of the parabola? Explain.

e. Could $y = x - 2$ be the equation of the parabola? Explain.

f. Does the line $y = -6$ intersect the parabola? Explain.

21. The profit P from a car wash held by the Metropolis Middle School band depends on the number of cars C that drive by the corner where the car wash is operated. Past experience suggests that the equation modeling the situation is approximately $P = 0.001C(C - 5)$.

a. What profit can be expected if 100 cars drive by?

b. What profit can be expected if 1000 cars drive by?

c. What profit can be expected if no cars drive by? Explain why the profit predicted by the equation does or does not make sense.

d. The band director estimates from past car washes that about 750 cars will drive by during the time the car wash is open. The band needs $700 to fund a trip to the state competition. About how many times will they have to hold the car wash to raise the necessary funds? Explain your reasoning.

22. The height h in meters of a model rocket t seconds after it is launched is approximated by the equation $h = t(50 - 3t)$.

a. How high is the rocket 5 seconds after being launched?

b. How high is the rocket 10 seconds after being launched?

c. Based on your answers to parts (a) and (b), did the rocket's height continue to increase after the first 5 seconds? Explain.

d. What is the height of the rocket after 17 seconds? What can you conclude from your answer? Explain.

Additional Practice *(continued)*

23. The sum of the length and width of a rectangle is 20 meters. The area of the rectangle is given by the equation $A = w(20 - w)$, where w is the width.

a. What is the area of the rectangle if the width is 2 meters?

b. What is the area of the rectangle if the length is 8 meters? Show how you found your answer.

c. Suppose the area of the rectangle is 75 square meters. What is the width of the rectangle? What is the length of the rectangle?

d. Suppose the area of the rectangle is 96 square meters. What is the width of the rectangle? What is the length of the rectangle?

e. What are the dimensions of the rectangle if its area is 93.75 square meters?

Additional Practice *(continued)*

24. Below is the graph of $y = (x + 3)(x - 2)$. The scale on both axes is 1.

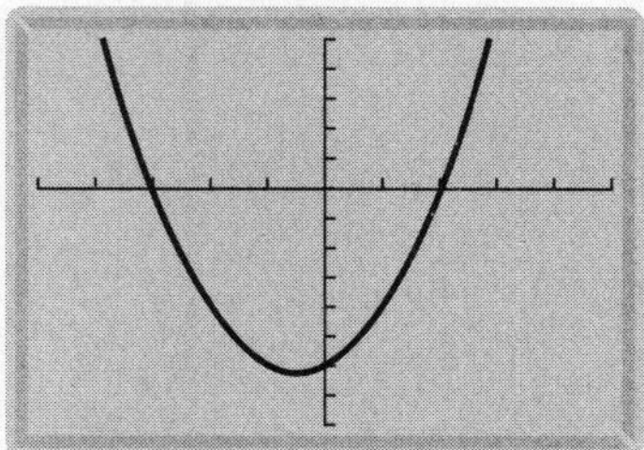

a. What is the solution to $(x + 3)(x - 2) = 0$? How is the solution shown on the graph?

b. What values of x satisfy the inequality $(x + 3)(x - 2) < 0$? How is your answer shown on the graph?

c. How can you find the answer to part (b), without using the graph, by analyzing the inequality? (Hint: Use what you know about multiplying positive and negative numbers.)

25. At right are graphs of four linear equations and their equations are given below. Match each equation with its graph and give reasons for your choices.

a. $y = 0.5x + 3$

b. $y = -0.5x + 6$

c. $y = 0.5x + 6$

d. $y = -0.5x + 3$

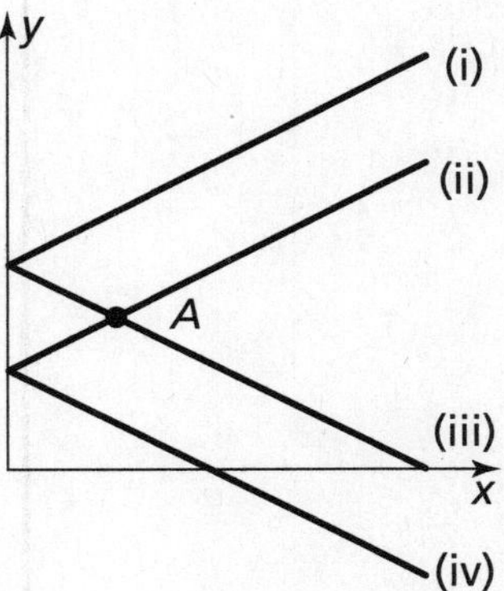

Name ______________________________ Date __________ Class __________

Skill: Solving Linear Equations

Solve and check each equation for the indicated variable.

1. $2(n-7) + 3 = 9$

2. $0 = 5(k + 9)$

3. $4h + 7h - 16 = 6$

4. $3(2n - 7) = 9$

5. $-27 = 8x - 5x$

6. $4p + 5 - 7p = -1$

7. $7 - y + 5y = 9$

8. $8e + 3(5 - e) = 10$

Skill: Solving Linear Equations *(continued)*

Solve each equation for the indicated variable.

9. $3k + 16 = 5k$

10. $5e = 3e + 36$

11. $n + 4n - 22 = 7n$

12. $2(x - 7) = 3x$

13. $8h - 10h = 3h + 25$

14. $7n + 6n - 5 = 4n + 4$

15. $y + 2(y - 5) = 2y + 2$

16. $-9x + 7 = 3x + 19$

Name ______________________ Date ___________ Class ___________

Skill: Factoring Quadratic Equations

Write each of these quadratic expressions in equivalent factored form.

1. $x^2 - 8x + 12$

2. $x^2 + 7x - 18$

3. $n^2 - 7n + 10$

4. $s^2 - 5s - 14$

5. $2x^2 + 3x + 1$

6. $3x^2 - x - 4$

7. $5x^2 - 2x - 7$

8. $3y^2 - 16y - 12$

9. $x^2 - 9$

10. $n^2 - 4$

11. $a^2 - 25$

12. $a^2 - 100$

Name ______________________ Date __________ Class __________

Skill: Solving Quadratic Equations

Solve each equation for x without using a table or graph.

1. $(x + 5)(x - 3) = 0$
2. $(x - 2)(x + 9) = 0$
3. $(b - 12)(b + 12) = 0$

Solve each equation for x by factoring.

4. $x^2 + 5x + 6 = 0$
5. $b^2 - 7b - 18 = 0$
6. $r^2 - 4 = 0$

Solve each equation for x.

7. $(x - 9)(x + 8) = 0$
8. $x^2 - 9x - 10 = 0$
9. $(c - 21)(c + 21) = 0$
10. $(x - 12)(5x - 13) = 0$
11. $2a^2 - 21a - 65 = 0$
12. $x^2 + 6x - 91 = 0$

Name ______________________ Date __________ Class __________

Additional Practice

1. When Michael and his three friends go to the movies, they each either skate to the theater or ride a bike. The number of wheels in the group as they go to the theater is given by the equation $W = 8s + 2b$, where s is the number of friends skating and b is the number of friends biking.
   a. If Michael decides to skate and his friends decide to bike, how many wheels are in the group?
   b. If everyone decides to skate, how many wheels are in the group?
   c. In the equation $W = 8s + 2b$, explain why the variable s has a coefficient of 8 and the variable b has a coefficient of 2.
   d. Suppose that as Michael and his three friends go to the movies, there are 26 wheels in the group. How many are on skates and how many are riding a bike? Explain your reasoning.

2. A car is stopped at a red light. When the light turns green, the car begins moving forward. The distance in feet of the car from the light after t seconds is given by the equation $D = 4t^2$.
   a. How far is the car from the light after 5 seconds?
   b. How far is the car from the light after 10 seconds?
   c. How far is the car from the light at $t = 0$ seconds? Explain.

3. Susan has a piggy bank into which she puts only nickels. The amount of money in dollars D in the bank is given by $D = \frac{n}{20}$, where n is the number of nickels in the piggy bank.
   a. If Susan has 80 nickels in her piggy bank, how many dollars does she have?
   b. If Susan has 94 nickels in her piggy bank, how many dollars does she have?
   c. Based on your answers to parts (a) and (b), explain why the equation makes sense.

Additional Practice *(continued)*

4. George's car has a 20-gallon gas tank. On average, he can travel 22 miles per gallon. If M is the number of miles driven since the last fill-up, he can use this formula to find out how much gas is left in the gas tank: $G = 20 - \left(\frac{1}{22}\right) M$

a. Why does the value 22 appear in the denominator of the fraction?

b. Why does the computation "start" with the value 20?

c. If George has driven 100 miles since he filled the tank, how much gas is left in the tank?

d. After filling up the tank, how far can George drive and be left with 4 gallons in the tank?

e. The "low fuel" light comes on when there is 1 gallon left. How far can George drive after a fill-up before the "low fuel" light comes on?

5. Kathy has a motorcycle with a 4-gallon gas tank. On average, she can travel 60 miles per gallon.

a. If M is the number of miles driven since the last fill-up, what formula can she use to find out how much gas is left in the gas tank?

b. How did you decide how to use or not use the value 4 in the formula?

c. How did you decide how to use or not use the value 60 in the formula?

d. If Kathy has driven 100 miles since she filled the tank, how much gas is left in the tank?

e. The distance from Dallas to Houston is 246 miles. Will she need to fill up on that trip?

Name ______________________ Date ____________ Class ____________

Skill: Nonlinear Functions

Investigation 4

Say It With Symbols

Complete the table for each function. Then graph the function.

1. $y = x^2 + 1$

x	$x^2 + 1 = y$
−3	
−2	
−1	
0	
1	
2	
3	

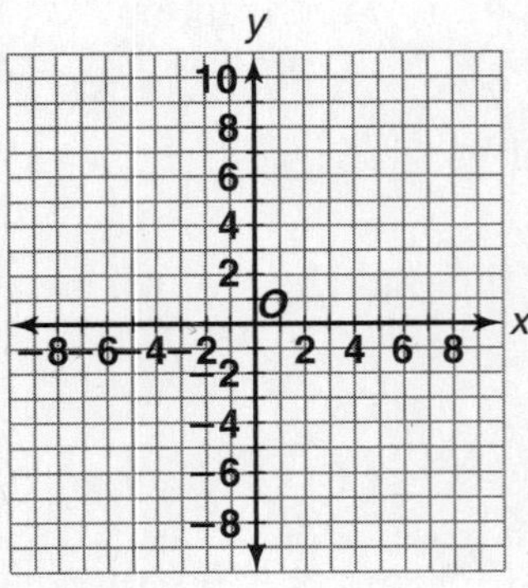

2. $y = 4 - x^2$

x	$4 - x^2 = y$
−3	
−2	
−1	
0	
1	
2	
3	

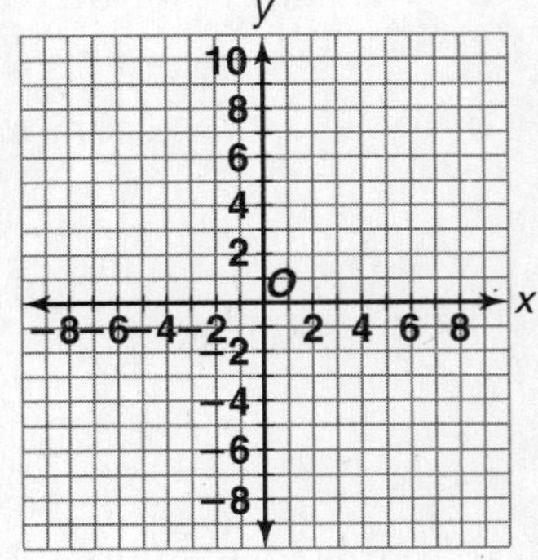

3. $y = \frac{20}{x}$

x	y
2	
4	
5	
10	

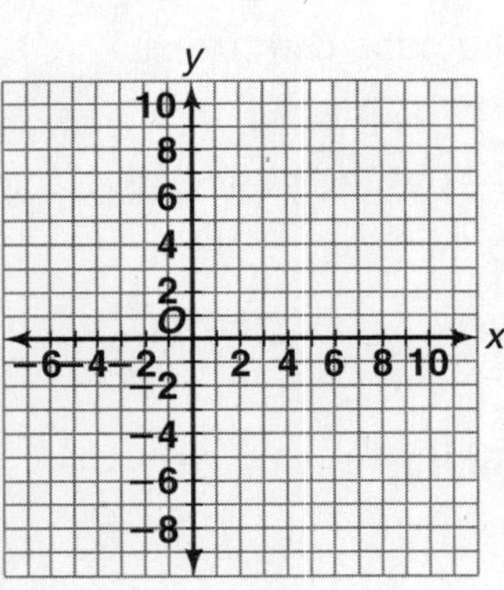

4. $y = 2^x - 1$

x	y
−1	
0	
1	
2	
3	

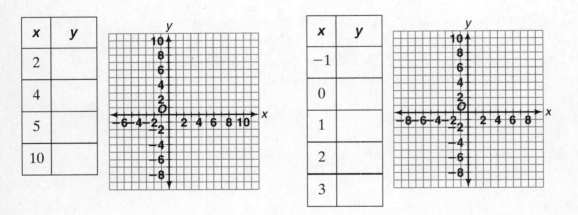

Does the point (2, 2) lie on the graph of each function?

5. $y = 2x - 2$ **6.** $y = \left(\frac{1}{2}\right)^x$ **7.** $y = x^2 - x$ **8.** $y = \frac{4}{x}$

Name ______________________________ Date ____________ Class ____________

Additional Practice

1. Show why this puzzle works:

Pick a number.

Add 5

Multiply by 2.

Divide by 10.

Subtract 1.

Multiply by 5

Your result is the number you picked at the beginning.

2. Show why this puzzle works:

Pick a number.

Multiply by 4

Add 6.

Divide by 2.

Divide by 2 again.

Subtract the number you started with.

Add $\frac{1}{2}$.

Your answer is 2.

3. Bill thinks that when you add two whole numbers each of which is divisible by 3, the sum is also divisible by 3. Is he right? Explain.

4. Susan thinks that when you add two whole numbers each of which is divisible by 6, the sum is divisible by 2 and by 3. Is she right? Explain.

5. Gene thinks that any whole number ending in 00 is divisible by 4 and any whole number ending in 000 is divisible by 8. Is he right? Explain.

6. Show that the square of an even number is divisible by 4.

7. Show that the square of a number divisible by 3 is divisible by 9.

Name ______________________ Date ____________ Class ____________

Additional Practice

1. The circle on the grid below has a radius of 20 and is centered at the origin. Use the drawing to help answer the following questions.

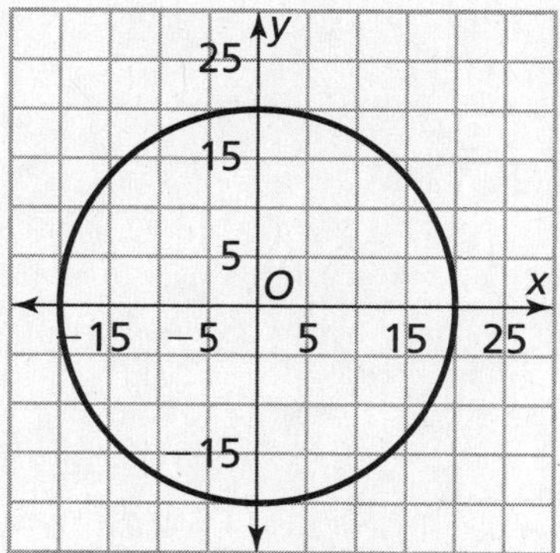

a. Write an equation that relates coordinates x and y for points on the circle.

b. Complete these ordered pairs so that the results describe points on the circle. Show how you know that each result satisfies the equation of the circle.

(4, □) (2, □) (−4, □)

(0, □) (□, −4) (□, −2)

(□, 0) (□, 3)

Name ______________________ Date ____________ Class ____________

Additional Practice *(continued)*

2. Find two equations of lines that are parallel to the lines with these equations.

a. $y = 3x + 9$

b. $y = -5x + 6$

c. $y = -7x + 8$

d. $y = \frac{3}{4}x - 22$

e. $y = -\frac{5}{7}x - 7$

f. $y = 3x - 4$

3. Find two equations of lines that are perpendicular to the lines with these equations.

a. $y = 3x + 7$

b. $y = -\frac{5}{6}x - 2$

c. $y = -5x + 8$

d. $y = 3x - 2$

e. $y = \frac{3}{4}x + 3$

f. $y = -4x - 3$

4. Find the coordinates of the midpoints of the segments with the following endpoints.

a. $(0, 0)$ and $(5, 15)$

b. $(2, 4)$ and $(6, -5)$

c. $(3, 5)$ and $(7, 5)$

d. $(0, 4)$ and $(0, -6)$

e. $(1, 1)$ and $(-6, -2)$

f. $(0, -5)$ and $(-1, -2)$

Name ______________________ Date __________ Class __________

Skill: Writing Linear Equations

Investigation 1

The Shapes of Algebra

Write an equation for the line with the given slope and *y*-intercept.

1. slope = 4, *y*-intercept = 8

2. slope = −2, *y*-intercept = −6

3. slope = $\frac{4}{3}$, *y*-intercept = 0

4. slope = $-\frac{9}{5}$, *y*-intercept = −7

5. slope = −6, *y*-intercept = 1

6. slope = $\frac{3}{7}$, *y*-intercept = −1

Name ______________________ Date __________ Class __________

Skill: Writing Linear Equations *(continued)*

Write an equation for the line through the given points or through the given point with the given slope.

7. $(5, 7), (6, 8)$

8. $(-2, 3)$; slope $= -1$

9. $(1, 2), (3, 8)$

10. $(6, -2)$; slope $= -\frac{4}{3}$

11. $(0, 5), (-3, 2)$

12. $(8, 11), (6, 16)$

Name ______________________ Date ___________ Class ___________

Skill: Parallel and Perpendicular Lines

Find an equation of a line that is parallel to the line of each equation.

1. $y = 2x - 7$

2. $y = -4x + 5$

3. $y = x - 3$

4. $y = \frac{3}{2}x + 9$

5. $y = -\frac{3}{4}x + 5$

6. $-7x - 3y = 3$

Skill: Parallel and Perpendicular Lines *(continued)*

Find the equation of a line that is perpendicular to the line of each equation.

7. $y = 3x - 2$

8. $y = -5x + 9$

9. $y = \frac{1}{6}x + 1$

10. $y = -\frac{1}{4}x + 7$

11. $y = 4x + 1$

12. $y = -\frac{4}{3}x - 7$

Name ______________________ Date __________ Class __________

Skill: Pythagorean Theorem and Midpoints

Find the missing length. If necessary, round the answer to the nearest tenth.

1. 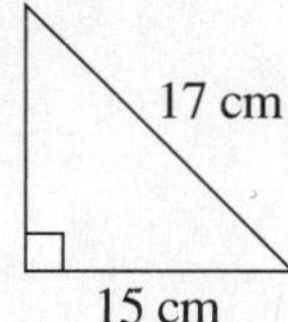

2. 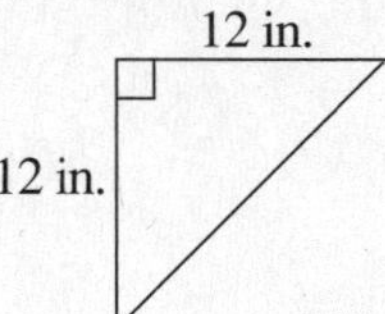

3. 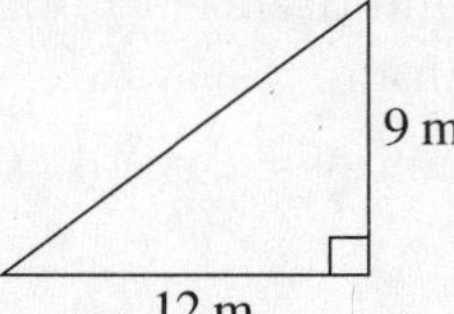

4. 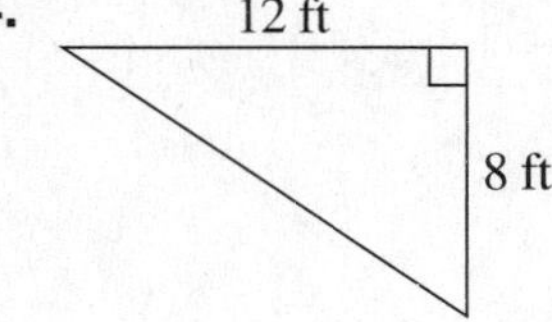

5. 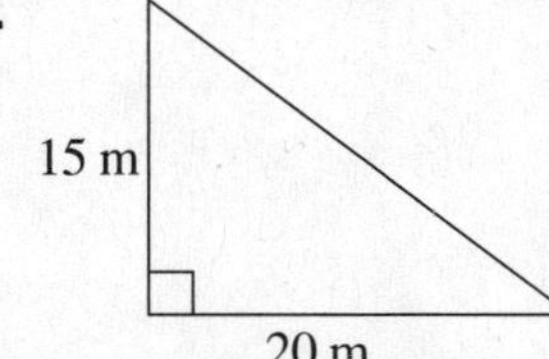

6. 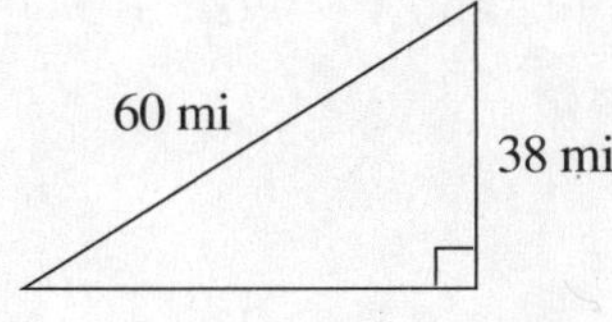

Find the coordinates of the midpoint of $\overline{XY}$.

7. $X(8, 14)$ and $Y(2, 6)$

8. $X(11, 7)$ and $Y(3, 19)$

9. $X(-7, 6)$ and $Y(11, -2)$

10. $X(-3, -2)$ and $Y(7, 8)$

11. $X(-4, -1)$ and $Y(-8, 5)$

12. $X(6, 15)$ and $Y(4, 8)$

Additional Practice

1. Graph the following pairs of equations on a coordinate grid. For each graph, estimate the point of intersection. Then use symbolic reasoning to see if your estimate is accurate.

   a. $y = 3x + 6$ and $y = \frac{1}{2}x - 4$

   b. $y = x + 2$ and $y = -2x + 3$

   c. $y = 5$ and $y = 10x - 5$

   d. $x = 0$ and $y = x + 7$

   e. $x = 7$ and $y = -5$

Additional Practice *(continued)*

2. Suppose that S and T are two numbers so that $S \geq T$. Which of the following inequalities are certainly true?

a. $S + 7 \geq T + 7$

b. $S - (-15) \geq T - (-15)$

c. $S \times 0 \geq T \times 0$

d. $\frac{S}{-2} \geq \frac{T}{-2}$

e. $\frac{S}{0.25} \geq \frac{T}{0.25}$

f. $S \times -2 \leq T \times -2$

g. $S + 7 \geq T + 5$

h. $S + 5 \geq T + 7$

3. Solve the following inequalities. Then create number line graphs for each solution.

a. $14 < 6x - 4$

b. $3x + 12 > 36$

c. $5x - 15 < 30$

d. $-8x - 10 > 18 - 16x$

4. The next diagram shows graphs of four linear functions: $y = 1.4x - 1$; $y = -2.4x + 1$; $y = 1$; and $y = -1$. Use the graph to estimate solutions for each of the given inequalities. Then use symbolic reasoning to check your estimates.

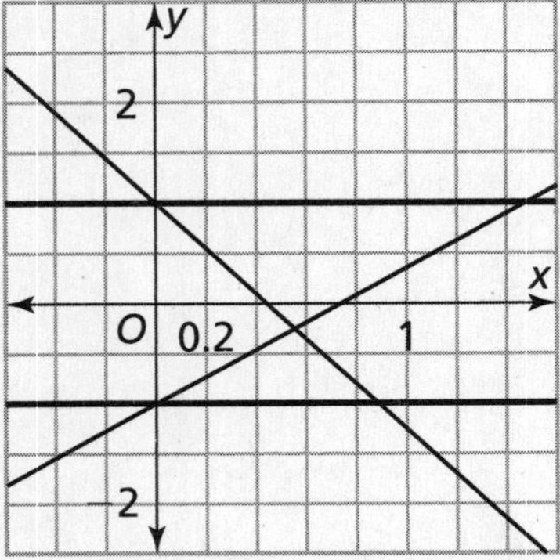

a. $1.4x - 1 > 1$

b. $1.4x - 1 > -1$

c. $-2.4x + 1 < -1$

d. $-2.4x + 1 = 1.4x - 1$

e. $-2.4x + 1 > 1.4x - 1$

Name ____ Date ____________ Class ____________

Skill: Solving Linear Systems

Investigation 2

The Shapes of Algebra

Graph the pairs of equations. For each graph estimate the point of intersection.

1. $y = x + 2$
$y = 2x + 1$

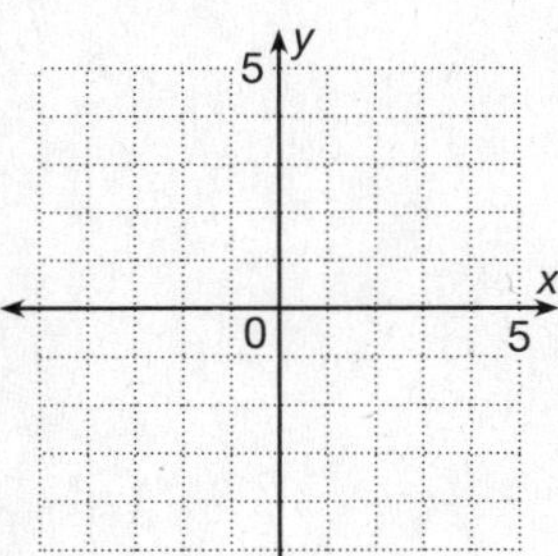

2. $y = -2x + 2$
$y = 3x + 2$

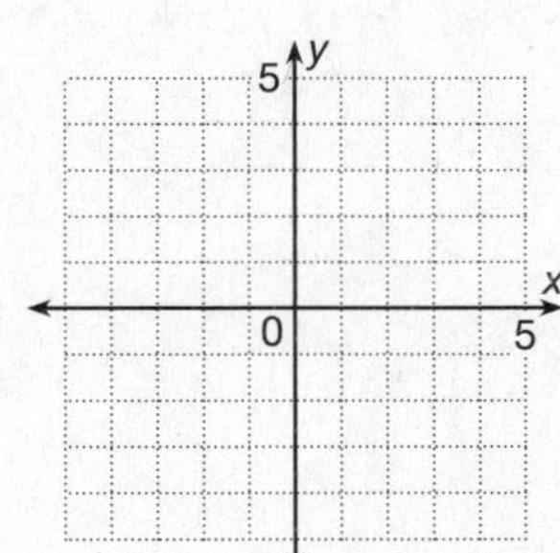

3. $y = -\frac{1}{2}x - 1$
$y = x - 4$

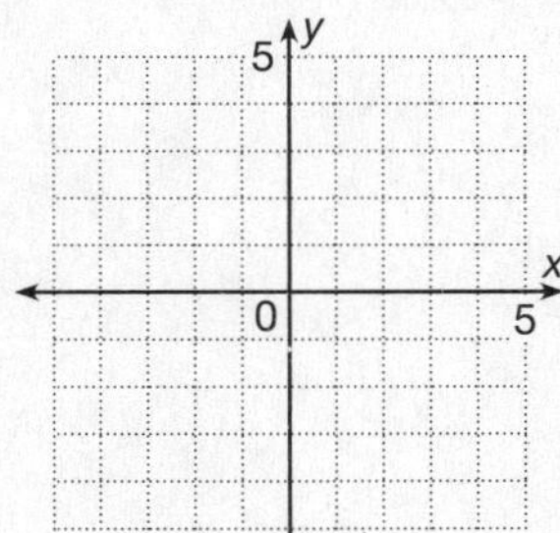

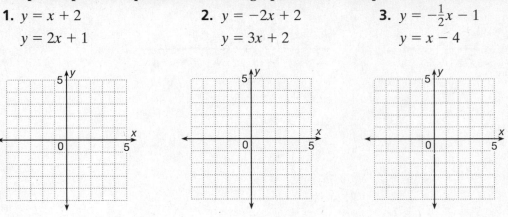

4. $y = 2x + 3$
$y = \frac{1}{2}x$

5. $y = -\frac{3}{2}x + 2$
$y = \frac{1}{2}x - 2$

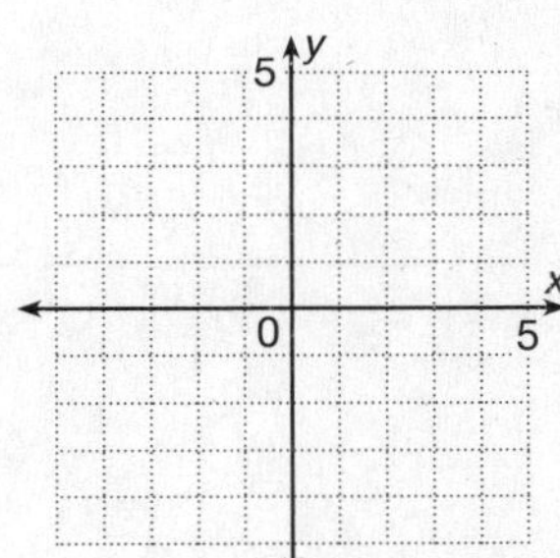

6. $y = 2x - 5$
$y = \frac{1}{4}x + 2$

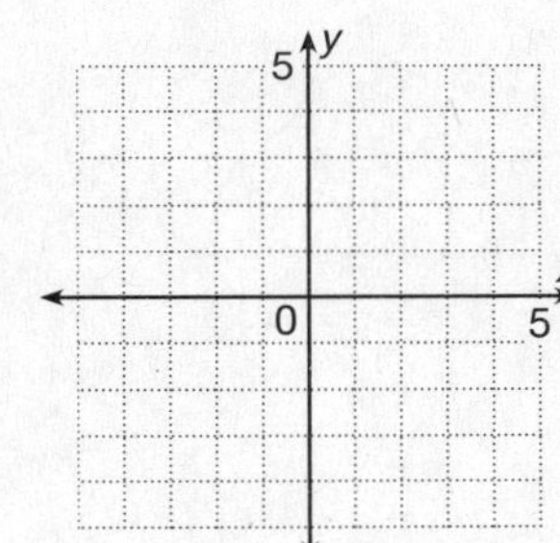

Name ______________________ Date __________ Class __________

Skill: Solving Linear Inequalities

Investigation 2

The Shapes of Algebra

Solve each inequality. Graph the solutions on the number line.

1. $m + 6 > 2$

−8 −7 −6 −5 −4 −3 −2 −1 0

2. $q + 4 \leq 9$

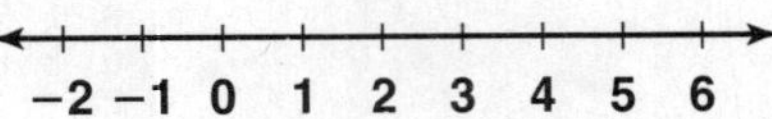

3. $w - 6 > -9$

−8 −7 −6 −5 −4 −3 −2 −1 0

4. $y - 3 < -4$

−6 −5 −4 −3 −2 −1 0 1 2

5. $-5m < 20$

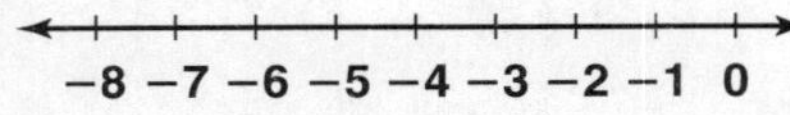

6. $\frac{j}{6} \leq 0$

−4 −3 −2 −1 0 1 2 3 4

7. $4v > 16$

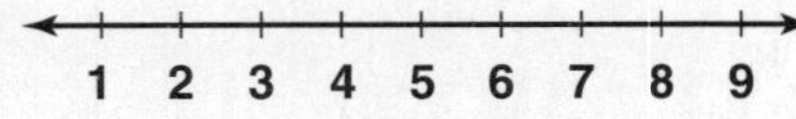

8. $\frac{b}{2} < 4$

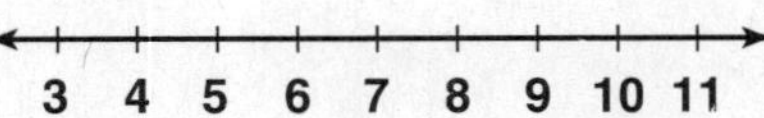

Skill: Solving Linear Inequalities *(continued)*

Solve each inequality.

9. $6x + 5 \leq -19$

10. $2x + 12 < 24$

11. $15x - 9 > 21$

12. $5x - 11 \geq -36$

13. $18x - 6 \geq 84$

14. $9x + 2.3 > -10.3$

Write and solve an inequality to answer each question.

15. A drama club's production of "Oklahoma!" is going to cost $1,250 to produce. How many tickets will they need to sell for $8 each in order to make a profit of at least $830?

16. A pet store is selling hamsters for $3.50 each if you purchase a cage for $18.25. You have at most $30 you can spend. How many hamsters can you buy?

Additional Practice

1. Marcello is an artist who makes oil paintings and charcoal sketches. He sells each oil painting for \$500 and each charcoal sketch for \$300.

   a. What equation shows Marcello's income I from the number of oil paintings x he sells and the number of charcoal sketches y he sells?

   b. Find Marcello's income from selling his art if he sells:

      i. 10 oil paintings and 5 charcoal sketches

      ii. 12 oil paintings and 4 charcoal sketches

      iii. 6 oil paintings and 12 charcoal sketches

   c. Find three pairs of numbers of oil paintings and charcoal sketches that will bring Marcello an income of \$20,000.

   d. Each answer in part (c) can be given as an ordered pair of numbers.

      i. Plot the points determined by those ordered pairs on a coordinate graph.

      ii. Use the graph of part (i) to estimate three other pairs of numbers that might allow the goal to be met.

   e. Write an equation relating numbers of oil paintings and the number of charcoal sketches Marcello must sell in order to make exactly \$20,000.

   f. Suppose Marcello wants to make 56 works in total. What equation relates the number of paintings x and the number of charcoals y to that goal?

   g. i. Graph the equations you found in parts (e) and (f).

      ii. Find the coordinates of the intersection point of the graphs. What does that intersection point tell us about how many paintings and how many charcoals Marcello should make?

Additional Practice *(continued)*

2. The students at Susan B. Anthony Middle School wanted to encourage people to buy tickets to the spring musical early. Tickets purchased at the door cost $6, and tickets purchased in advance only cost $4. Receipts from ticket sales totaled $2,000 and there were 410 tickets sold.

a. Use x to represent the number of tickets sold at the door and y to represent the number of tickets sold in advance. Write a system of equations that represent the reported information about receipts from ticket sales and the total number of tickets.

b. Graph the equations you found in part (a).

c. Use your graph to find the number of tickets sold at the door and the number of tickets sold in advance.

3. For the following equations identify the slope and y-intercept and then write the equation in equivalent $ax + by = c$ form.

a. $y = 3x$ **b.** $y = -2x + 12$ **c.** $y = x - 10$

d. $y = 0$ **e.** $y = -2x - 4$ **f.** $y = -x - 2$

4. Write the following equations in $y = mx + b$ form and then identify the slope and y-intercept.

a. $-5x - y = -2$ **b.** $x = -9$ **c.** $x - y = 20$

d. $x + y = 12$ **e.** $-x + 5y = -20$ **f.** $2x - 3y = 25$

Skill: Writing Equations With Two Variables

1. The drama club sells 200 lb of fruit to raise money. The fruit is sold in 5-lb bags and 10-lb bags.
   a. Write an equation to find the number of each type of bag that the club should sell.
   b. Graph your equation to the right.
   c. Use your graph to find two different solution pairs for the equation.

2. The student council is sponsoring a carnival to raise money. Tickets cost $5 for adults and $3 for students. The student council wants to raise $450.
   a. Write an equation to find the number of each type of ticket they should sell.
   b. Graph your equation to the right.
   c. Use your graph to find two different solution pairs for the equation.

3. Anna goes to a store to buy $70 worth of flour and sugar for her bakery. A bag of flour costs $5, and a bag of sugar costs $7.
   a. Write an equation to find the number of bags of each type Anna can buy.
   b. Graph your equation to the right.

4. You have $50 to spend on cold cuts for a party. Ham costs $5.99/lb, and turkey costs $4.99/lb. Write an equation to relate the number of pounds of each kind of meat you could buy.

Name ______________________________ Date __________ Class __________

Skill: Standard Form and Slope-Intercept Form

Write each equation in $y = mx + b$ form.

1. $3y = 15x - 12$

2. $5x + 10 = 10y$

3. $3y - 21 = 12x$

4. $5y + 3 = 2y - 3x + 5$

5. $-2(x + 3y) = 18$

6. $5(x + y) = 20 + 5x$

Name ______________________ Date __________ Class __________

Skill: Standard Form and Slope-Intercept Form (cont.)

Write each equation in $ax + by = c$ form.

7. $y = 4x - 11$

8. $y = 2x - 6$

9. $y = -2x - 3$

10. $y = 5x - 32$

11. $y = \frac{2}{3}x - \frac{25}{3}$

12. $y = 43 - 4x$

13. $y = -\frac{4}{5}x + \frac{6}{5}$

14. $y = -\frac{x}{5}$

Name ________________________ Date ____________ Class ____________

Skill: Solving Linear Systems

Use graphing methods to find solutions for these systems of linear equations.

1. $2x + y = 1$
$x - 2y = 3$

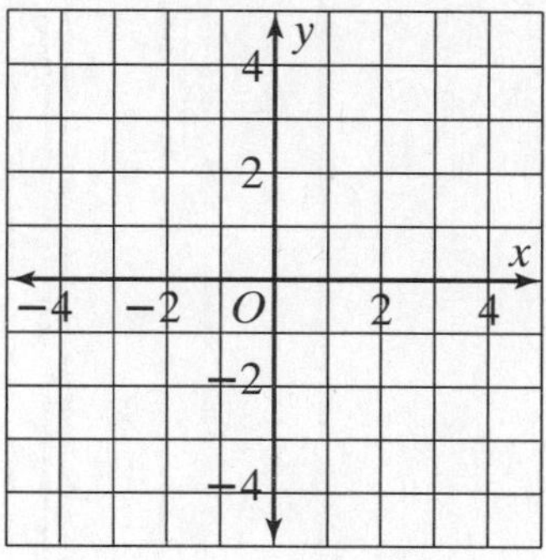

2. $y + 2 = 0$
$2x + y = 0$

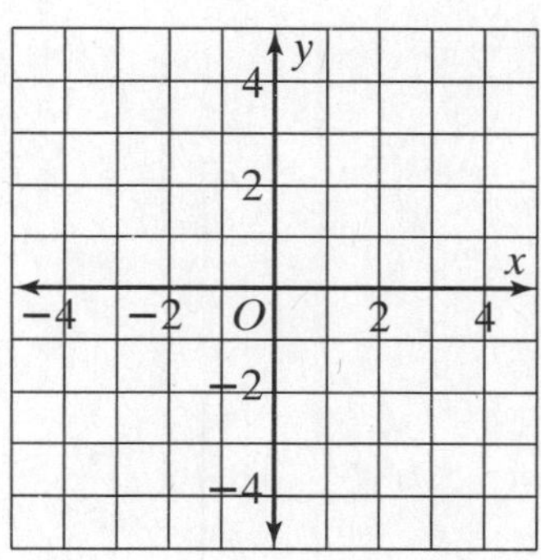

3. $3x + 2y = -6$
$x + 3y = -2$

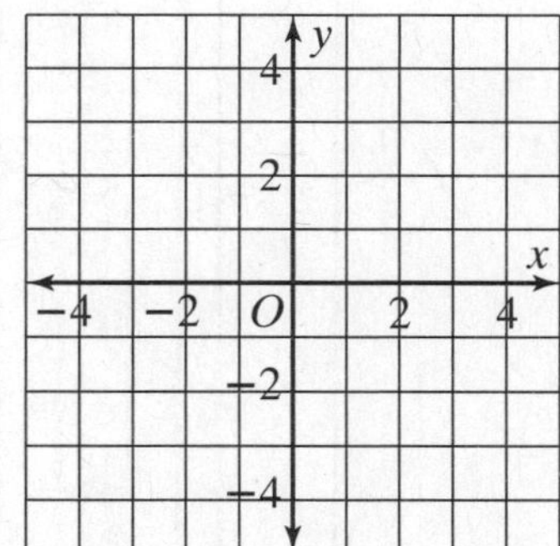

Additional Practice

1. Solve each of the following systems of equations.

a. $y = 3x - 2$
$y = 2x + 3$

b. $y = 7x + 4$
$y = 9x - 6$

c. $y = 22x + 4$
$y = 14x + 28$

d. $y = -x + 9$
$y = 2x + 30$

e. $y = 2x + 6$
$y = x + 3$

f. $y = -5x + 8$
$y = -2x - 7$

Additional Practice *(continued)*

2. Rewrite the following equations in equivalent $y = mx + b$ form:

a. $2x + 3y + 6 = 0$

b. $-5x + 10y + 15 = 0$

c. $-6x - 2y - 3 = 0$

d. $-4x + y = 0$

e. $4x - 4y + 2 = 0$

f. $150x + 50y - 25 = 0$

3. Rewrite each of the equations in Exercise 2 in equivalent $x = ny + c$ form.

4. Solve each of the following systems of equations by substitution.

a. $3x + 2y = 14$

$y = x + 2$

b. $4x - 2y = 24$

$y = x - 5$

c. $-3x + 51 = 8y$

$y = -6x$

d. $y = 4x - 2$

$3x + 2y = -4$

e. $x = 5y - 26$

$6x + y = -1$

f. $7x - 2y = 18$

$x = y$

Additional Practice *(continued)*

5. Solve each of the following systems of equations by combination.

a. $2x - 4y = 10$
$-2x + 6y = -4$

b. $7x + 10y = 6$
$7x - 10y = 8$

c. $6x - 7y = -4$
$-4x - 7y = 26$

d. $x + y = 3$
$x - y = -9$

e. $-5x - 6y = 16$
$-5x + 8y = 4$

f. $3x - 2y = 12$
$-3x + 4y = -8$

Name ______________________________ Date ____________ Class ____________

Skill: Substitution Method for Linear Systems

Investigation 4

The Shapes of Algebra

Solve each system of equations using substitution.

1. $y = x$
$y = -x + 2$

2. $y = x + 4$
$y = 3x$

3. $x = -2y + 1$
$x = y - 5$

4. $x + 2y = 200$
$x = y + 50$

Name ______________________________ Date __________ Class __________

Skill: Substitution Method for Linear Systems *(cont.)*

Solve each system of equations using substitution.

5. $3x - 2y = 0$
$x + 2y = -5$

6. $2x + 4y = -6$
$x - 3y = -7$

7. $5x - 3y = -4$
$5x + 3y = -4$

8. $3x - y = 14$
$2x + y = 16$

Name ______________________________ Date ____________ Class ____________

Skill: Combination Method for Linear Systems

Solve each system of equations by combination.

1. $x + 2y = 7$
$3x - 2y = -3$

2. $3x + y = 20$
$x + y = 12$

3. $5x + 7y = 77$
$5x + 3y = 53$

4. $2x + 5y = -1$
$x + 2y = 0$

Skill: Combination Method for Linear Systems *(cont.)*

Solve each system of equations by combination.

5. $3x + 6y = 6$
$2x - 3y = 4$

6. $2x + y = 3$
$-2x + y = 1$

7. $4x - y = 6$
$3x + 2y = 21$

8. $2x - 3y = -11$
$3x + 2y = 29$

Name ______________________________ Date ___________ Class ___________

Additional Practice

Investigation 5

The Shapes of Algebra

1. Match each inequality a–i with its graph.

a. $x - 2y \geq 4$ **b.** $y - 2x \geq 4$ **c.** $2x + y \leq 4$

d. $x + 2y \leq 4$ **e.** $y \geq -2x$ **f.** $y \leq -2x$

g. $x \geq -2$ **h.** $y \geq -2$ **i.** $-2 < x$

i.

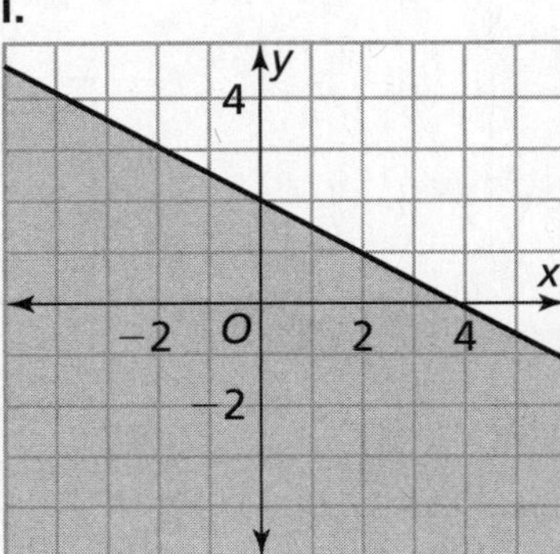

ii.

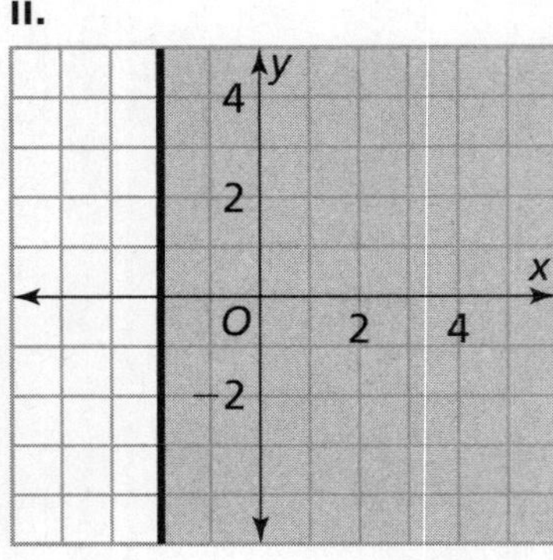

iii.

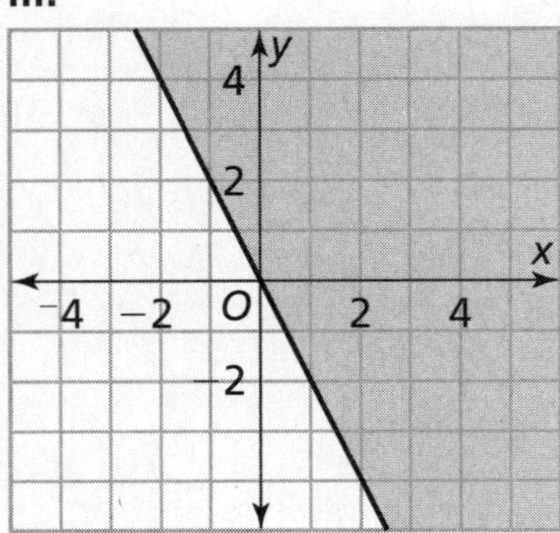

iv.

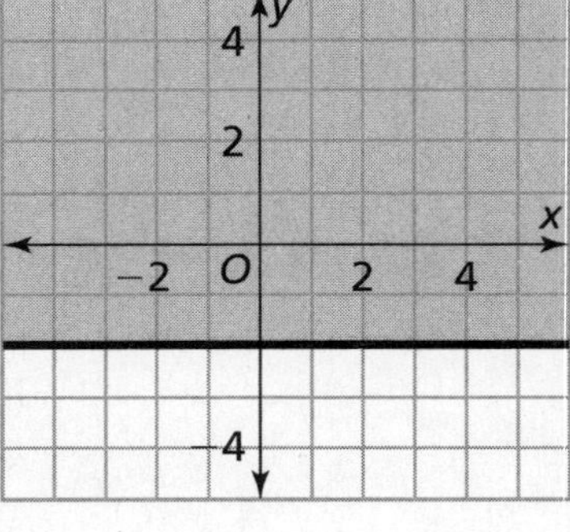

v.

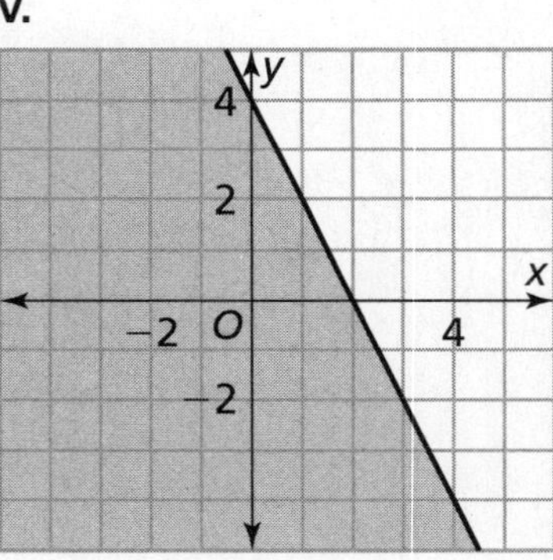

vi.

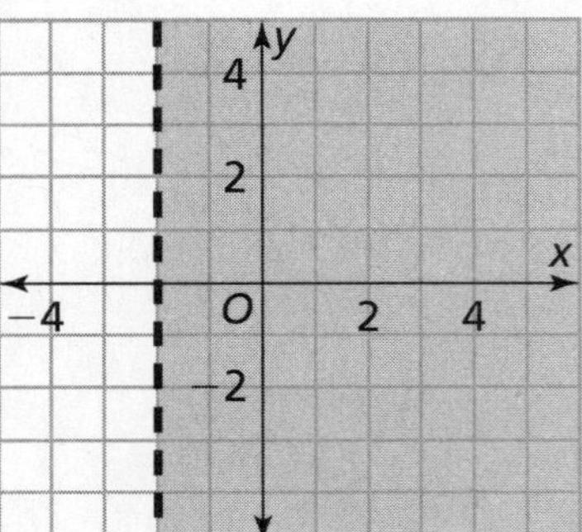

vii.

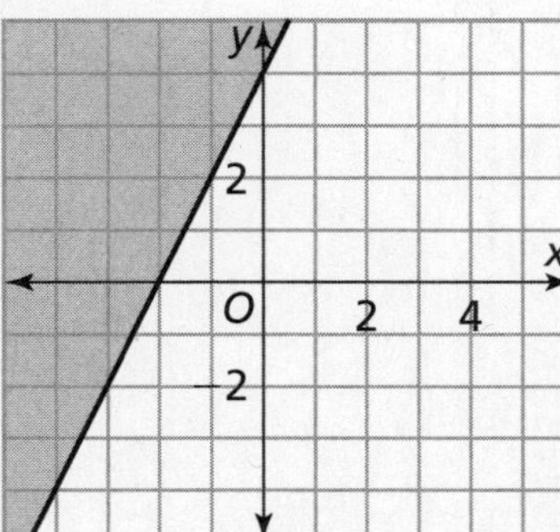

viii.

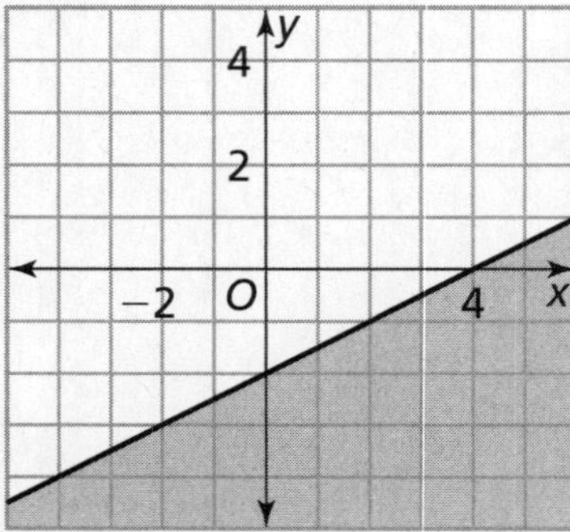

ix.

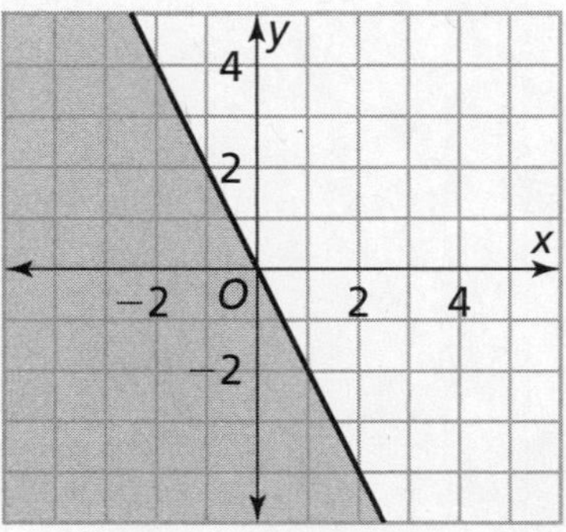

2. For each of the inequalities in parts (a)–(c):
   i. Find three solutions (x, y) that satisfy the inequality.
   ii. Find three solutions (x, y) that do NOT satisfy the inequality.
   iii. Draw a graph illustrating the solutions of the inequality.

   a. $x - 5y \geq 10$

   b. $5x - y \leq 10$

   c. $x - 5y < 10$

Additional Practice *(continued)*

3. For each of the inequalities in parts (a)–(d), draw a graph illustrating the solutions of the inequality.

   a. $x \geq 6 + 3y$

   b. $x \geq 6$

   c. $y < -5$

   d. $3x - 6y \geq 9$

   e. What strategies did you use to draw the graphs in parts (a)–(d)?

Additional Practice *(continued)*

4. For each of the following systems of inequalities:

i. Find three coordinate pairs that are solutions to the system.

ii. Find three coordinate pairs that are not solutions to the system.

iii. Graph the solutions to the system.

a. $2x + 3y \geq 6$
$x + 4y \leq 10$

b. $3x - 5y \leq 0$
$x - y > -1$

Name ______________________________ Date __________ Class __________

Skill: Inequalities With Two Variables

1. Suppose your class is raising money for the Red Cross. You make \$5 on each basket of fruit and \$3 on each box of cheese that you sell. How many items of each type must you sell to raise more than \$150?

a. Write a linear inequality to model this condition.

b. Draw a graph of all the (fruit, cheese) pairs that satisfy this condition.

2. Suppose you intend to spend no more than \$60 buying books. Hardback books cost \$12 and paperbacks cost \$5. How many books of each type can you buy?

a. Write a linear inequality to model the situation.

b. Draw a graph of all the (hardback, paperback) pairs that satisfy this condition.

3. Suppose that for your exercise program, you either walk 5 miles per day or ride your bicycle 10 miles per day. How many days will it take you to cover a distance of at least 150 miles?

a. Write a linear inequality to model the situation.

b. Draw a graph of all the (walk, ride) pairs that satisfy this condition.

Name ______________________ Date ____________ Class ____________

Skill: Graphs of Linear Inequalities

Investigation 5

The Shapes of Algebra

Graph each inequality.

1. $y < x$

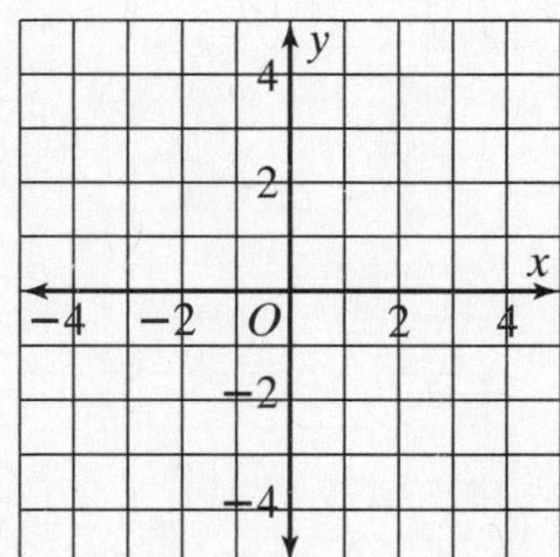

2. $x + y \leq 2$

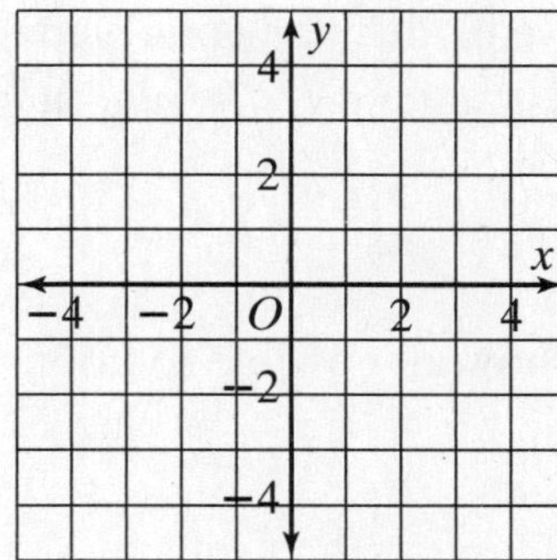

3. $x + 2y \geq 4$

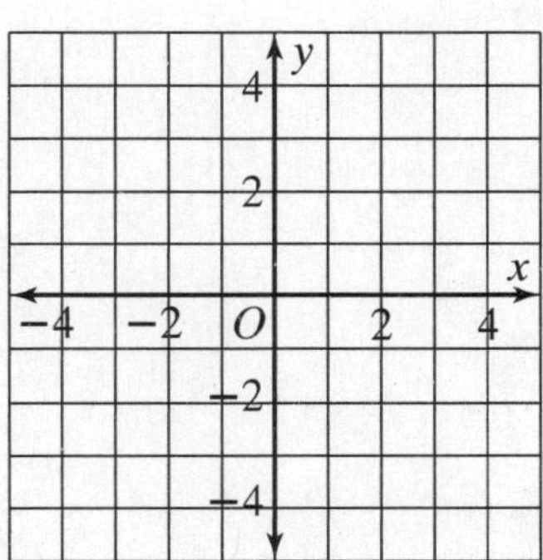

4. $x > -2$

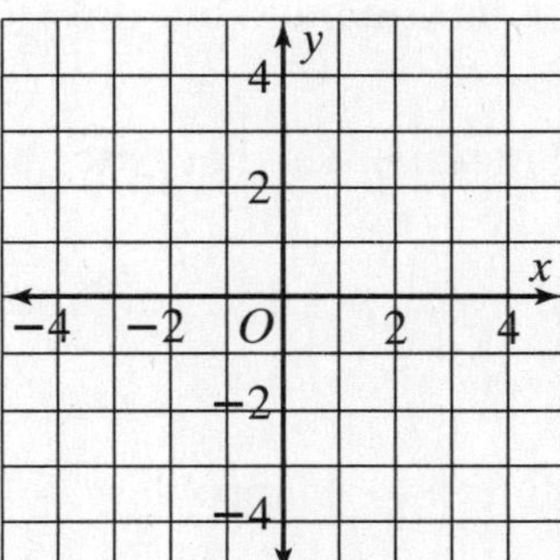

Name ______________________________ Date __________ Class __________

Skill: Systems of Linear Inequalities

Investigation 5

The Shapes of Algebra

1. In basketball you score 2 points for a field goal and 1 point for a free throw. Suppose that you have scored at least 3 points in every game this season, and have a season high score of 15 points in one game. How many field goals and free throws could you have made in any one game?

a. Write a system of two inequalities that describes this situation.

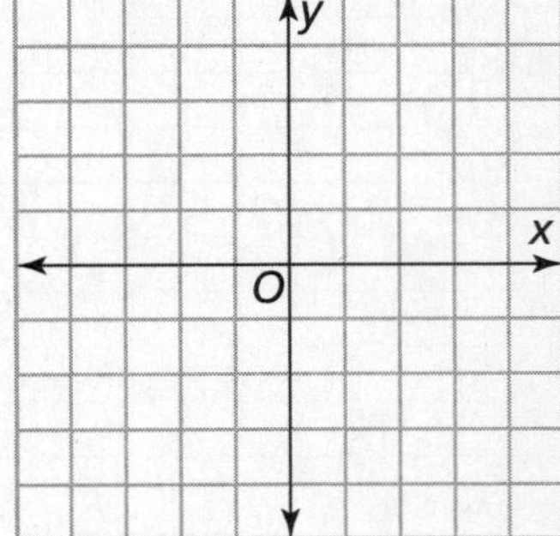

b. Graph the system to show all possible solutions.

c. Write one possible solution to the problem.

2. Suppose you need to use at least $1.00 worth of stamps to mail a package. You have as many $0.03 stamps as you need but only four $0.32 stamps. How many of each stamp can you use?

a. Write a system of two inequalities that describes this situation.

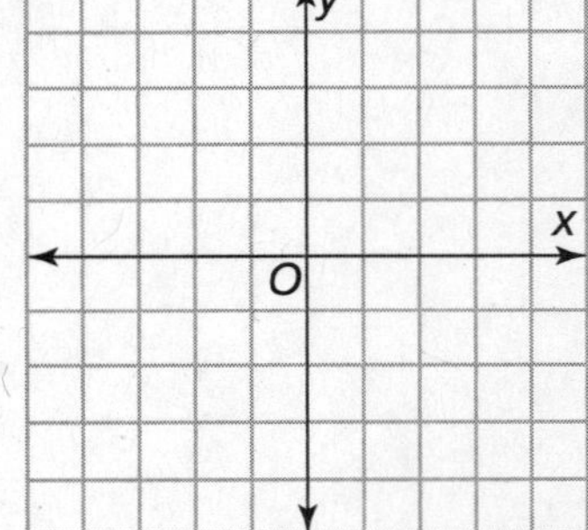

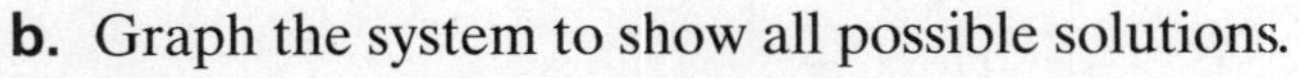

b. Graph the system to show all possible solutions.

c. Write one possible solution to the problem.

3. A grandmother wants to spend at least $40 but no more than $60 on school clothes for her grandson. T-shirts sell for $10 and pants sell for $20. How many T-shirts and pants could she buy?

a. Write a system of two inequalities that describes this situation.

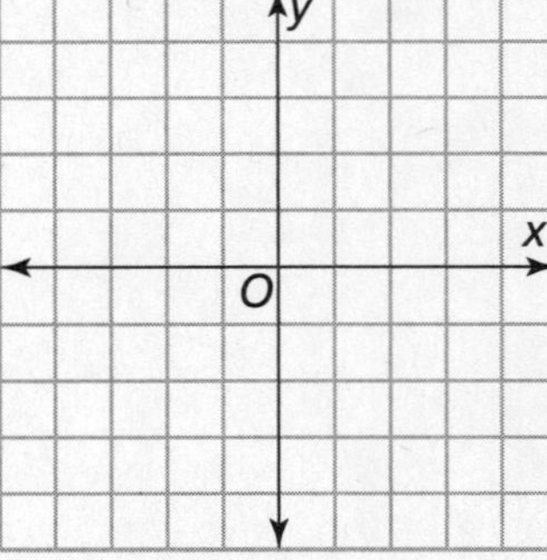

b. Graph the system to show all possible solutions.

c. Write two possible solutions to the problem.

Name ______________________ Date __________ Class __________

Additional Practice

Investigation 1

Samples and Populations

Another peanut butter survey was conducted more recently than the survey you studied in Investigation 1. The data for natural and regular brands are presented in the table.

Peanut Butter Comparisons

Brand	Quality Rating	Sodium per Serving (mg)	Price per Serving	Regular/ Natural	Creamy/ Chunky	Name Brand/ Store Brand
Arrowhead Mills	85	0	36	natural	creamy	name
Laura Scudder's (Southeast)	79	165	25	natural	creamy	name
Adams (West)	73	173	23	natural	creamy	name
Smucker's	73	180	26	natural	creamy	name
Nature's Cupboard (Safeway)	68	240	26	natural	creamy	store
Laura Scudder's Nutty (Southeast)	84	165	26	natural	chunky	name
Arrowhead Mills	83	0	37	natural	chunky	name
Smucker's	79	180	26	natural	chunky	name
Adams (West)	75	135	23	natural	chunky	name
Nature's Cupboard (Safeway)	72	195	26	natural	chunky	store
Jif	85	225	19	regular	creamy	name
Simply Jif	85	98	19	regular	creamy	name
Peter Pan	82	225	17	regular	creamy	name
Skippy	82	225	18	regular	creamy	name
Kroger	79	195	15	regular	creamy	store
Skippy Roasted Honey Nut	79	180	19	regular	creamy	name
America's Choice	77	225	17	regular	creamy	store
Reese's	68	173	19	regular	creamy	name
Townhouse (Safeway)	68	240	18	regular	creamy	store
Peter Pan Very Low Sodium	57	15	18	regular	creamy	name
Peter Pan Whipped	49	173	17	regular	creamy	name
Jif Extra Crunchy	88	195	19	regular	chunky	name
Skippy Super Chunk	87	210	19	regular	chunky	name
Peter Pan Extra Crunchy	86	180	17	regular	chunky	name
Reese's	86	120	19	regular	chunky	name
Skippy Roasted Honey Nut	86	180	19	regular	chunky	name
Kroger	84	195	15	regular	chunky	store
Simply Jif Extra Crunchy	83	75	19	regular	chunky	name
America's Choice Krunchy	80	188	17	regular	chunky	store
Townhouse (Safeway)	72	195	18	regular	chunky	store

Source: "Peanut Butter: It's Not Just for Kids Anymore." *Consumer Reports* (September 1995): pp. 576–579.

1. The box plots below show the quality ratings of natural versus regular brands, creamy versus chunky brands, and name brands versus store brands. Based on these box plots, what characteristics would you look for if you wanted to choose a peanut butter based on quality rating? Explain your reasoning.

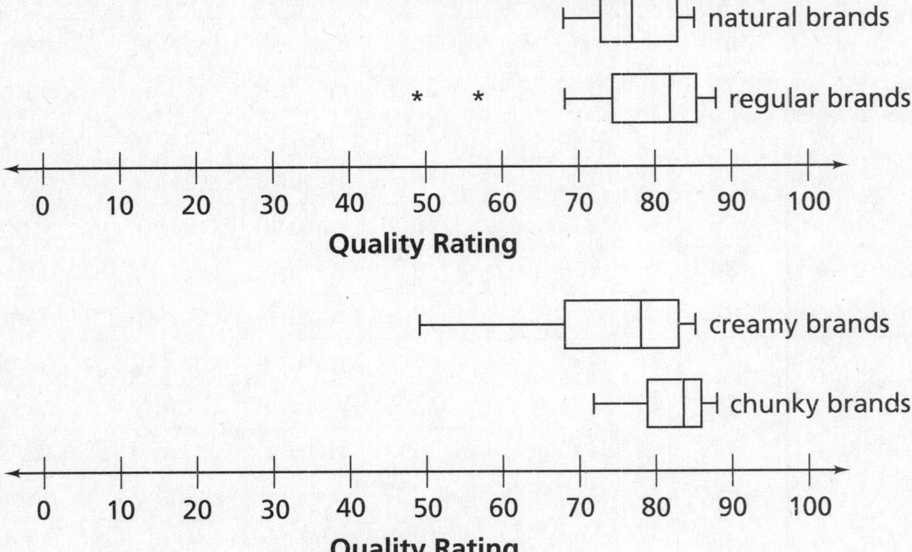

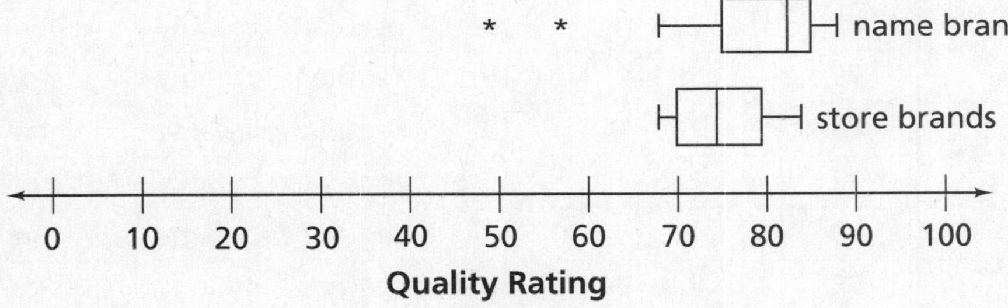

2. Make box plots to compare the peanut butters based on price. Mark any outliers with an asterisk (*). Which characteristic(s) help identify low-price peanut butters? Explain your reasoning.

Ms. Humphrey asked each of the 21 students in her class to choose a number between 1 and 50. Ms. Humphrey recorded the data and made this box plot:

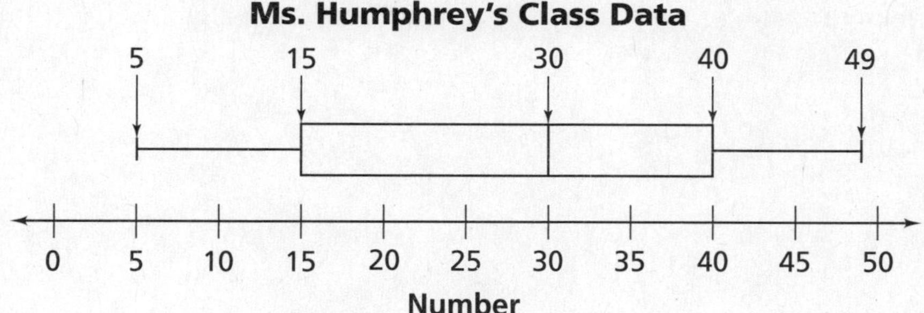

3. What is the median number that was chosen?

4. What percent of students in Ms. Humphrey's class chose numbers above 15? Explain your reasoning.

5. About how many students chose numbers between 30 and 40? Explain.

6. What were the least and the greatest numbers chosen?

7. Is it possible to determine from the box plot whether one of the students chose the number 27? Explain.

8. Is it possible to determine from the box plot whether one of the students chose the number 4? Explain.

Additional Practice *(continued)*

For Exercises 9–12, refer to the table on the next page.

9. Finish computing the values for the fifth column.

10. What does it mean when the ratio of wingspan to body length is 1? Greater than 1? Less than 1?

11. Compute the five-number summary for jet planes and the five-number summary for propeller planes of the ratio of wingspan to body length. Explain what the medians tell you about the relationship between wingspan and body length for jet planes and for propeller planes.

12. Make box plots from your five-number summaries. Explain what your plots reveal about how jet planes and propeller planes compare based on ratio of wingspan to body length.

Airplane Data

Plane	Engine Type	Body Length (m)	Wingspan (m)	Wingspan-to-Length Ratio
Boeing 707	jet	46.6	44.4	0.953
Boeing 747	jet	70.7	59.6	0.843
Ilyushin IL-86	jet	59.5	48.1	
McDonnell Douglas DC-8	jet	57.1	45.2	
Antonov An-124	jet	69.1	73.3	
British Aerospace 146	jet	28.6	26.3	
Lockheed C-5 Galaxy	jet	75.5	67.9	
Antonov An-225	jet	84.0	88.4	
Airbus A300	jet	54.1	44.9	
Airbus A310	jet	46.0	43.9	
Airbus A320	jet	37.5	33.9	
Boeing 737	jet	33.4	28.9	
Boeing 757	jet	47.3	38.1	
Boeing 767	jet	48.5	47.6	
Lockheed Tristar L-1011	jet	54.2	47.3	
McDonnell Douglas DC-10	jet	55.5	50.4	
Aero/Boeing Spacelines Guppy	propeller	43.8	47.6	
Douglas DC-4 C-54 Skymaster	propeller	28.6	35.8	
Douglas DC-6	propeller	32.2	35.8	
Lockheed L-188 Electra	propeller	31.8	30.2	
Vickers Viscount	propeller	26.1	28.6	
Antonov An-12	propeller	33.1	38.0	
de Havilland DHC Dash-7	propeller	24.5	28.4	
Lockheed C-130 Hercules/L-100	propeller	34.4	40.4	
British Aerospace 748/ATP	propeller	26.0	30.6	
Convair 240	propeller	24.1	32.1	
Curtiss C-46 Commando	propeller	23.3	32.9	
Douglas DC-3	propeller	19.7	29.0	
Grumman Gulfstream I/I-C	propeller	19.4	23.9	
Ilyushin IL-14	propeller	22.3	31.7	
Martin 4-0-4	propeller	22.8	28.4	
Saab 340	propeller	19.7	21.4	

Source: William Berk and Frank Berk. *Airport Airplanes*. Plymouth, Mich.: Plymouth Press, 1993.

Name ______________________________ Date __________ Class __________

Skill: Histograms

Investigation 1

Samples and Populations

1. Would the data below be better displayed on a histogram with 3-minute intervals or 5-minute intervals? Explain.

Time to Walk to School															
Time (min.)	1	2	3	4	5	6	7	8	9	10	11	12	13	14	15
Tally			II	IIII	III	IIII	I	II			I	I			I

2. Make a histogram for the time it takes the group of students in Exercise 1 to walk to school.

3. Make a histogram for the data. Use the intervals in the table.

Hours Spent Doing Homework

Number of Hours	Frequency
1 – 1.75	1
2 – 2.75	1
3 – 3.75	2
4 – 4.75	6
5 – 5.75	8
6 – 6.75	3
7 – 7.75	2
8 – 8.75	1

Name ________________________________ Date ____________ Class ____________

Skill: Box-and-Whisker Plots

Investigation 1

Samples and Populations

Use the box-and-whisker plot to find each value.

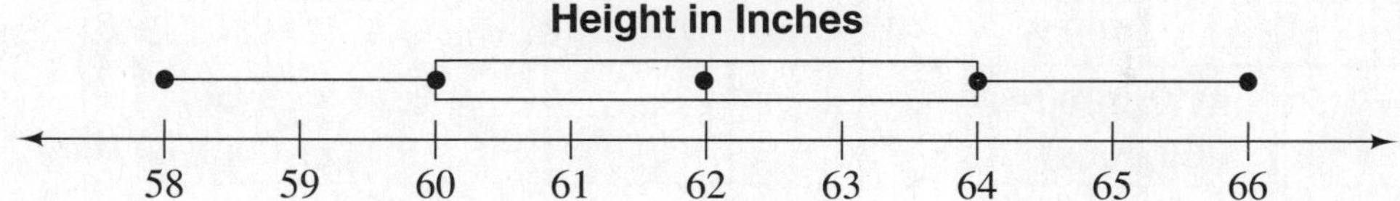

1. the median height

2. the lower quartile

3. the upper quartile

4. the greatest height

5. the shortest height

6. the range of heights

Name ______________________________ Date ____________ Class ____________

Skill: Box-and-Whisker Plots *(continued)*

Make a box-and-whisker plot for each set of data.

7.

Cargo Airlines in the U.S. (1991)	
Airline	**Freight ton-miles (1,000,000s)**
Federal Express	3,622
Northwest	1,684
United	1,214
American	884
Delta	668
Continental	564
Pan American	377
Trans World	369
United Parcel Service	210

8.

Immigration to the U.S. (1981–1990)	
Country	**Number (1,000s)**
Mexico	1,656
Philippines	549
China	347
Korea	334
Vietnam	281
Dominican Republic	252
India	251
El Salvador	214
Jamaica	208
United Kingdom	159

Use box-and-whisker plots to compare data sets. Use a single number line for each comparison.

9. 1st set: 7 12 25 3 1 29 30 7 15 2 5 10 29 1 10 30 18 8 7 29

2nd set: 37 17 14 43 27 19 32 1 8 48 26 16 28 6 25 18

0 5 10 15 20 25 30 35 40 45 50

1st Set

2nd Set

Name ________________________________ Date ____________ Class ____________

Additional Practice

Investigation 2

Aaron wants to learn about how much time students at his school spend playing sports. He asks all the boys on the basketball team and all the girls on the volleyball team to estimate how many hours per week they spend playing sports.

1. Is Aaron's sample a voluntary-response sample, a systematic sample, or a convenience sample? Explain your reasoning.

2. Suppose Aaron asked all the students in his mathematics class to estimate how many hours per week they spend playing sports.
   a. Would this be a voluntary-response sample, a systematic sample, or a convenience sample? Explain your reasoning.

   b. Would you expect the median number of hours spent playing sports for students in Aaron's mathematics class to be higher or lower than his sample from the basketball and volleyball teams? Explain your reasoning.

3. There are 1,232 students enrolled at Aaron's school. The principal's office has an alphabetical list of all the students' names. Suppose Aaron asked every 20th student on the list to estimate the number of hours he or she spends playing sports each week. Would this be a voluntary-response sample, a systematic sample, or a convenience sample? Explain.

4. Aaron placed an ad in the school newspaper with a form for students to complete and return. The form asked how much time the students spent playing sports each week. Aaron received 53 responses. Is this a voluntary-response sample, a systematic sample, or a convenience sample? Explain.

For Exercises 5–7, use this information: Marci works on the yearbook staff at Metropolis Middle School. Of the 92 businesses in the downtown area, 41 purchased advertising space in the yearbook last year.

5. Suppose Marci wants to investigate why businesses did not advertise in the yearbook last year. Describe a sampling strategy she could use to call 10 businesses.

6. Suppose Marci wants to investigate how satisfied advertisers are with yearbook ads. Describe a sampling strategy she could use to call 10 businesses.

7. Suppose Marci wants to investigate how likely a typical downtown business is to advertise in the upcoming yearbook. Describe a sampling strategy she could use to call 10 businesses.

8. The principal of a nearby school, Megalopolis Middle School, decided to conduct a survey of the 1,107 enrolled students. She asked three teachers how many students they thought should be surveyed. One teacher said to survey 200 girls and 100 boys, the second said to randomly select and survey 50 students, and the third said to survey the first 100 students to enter the building one morning next week.

a. Explain which of the three samples will produce data that may best represent all the students at Megalopolis.

b. Explain why you feel that the other two samples would not be as representative of all the students as the one you chose in part a.

In a survey of the cafeteria food at a middle school, 50 students were asked to rate how well they liked the lunches on a scale of 1 to 10, with 1 being the lowest rating and 10 being the highest rating. The box plot below was made from the collected data.

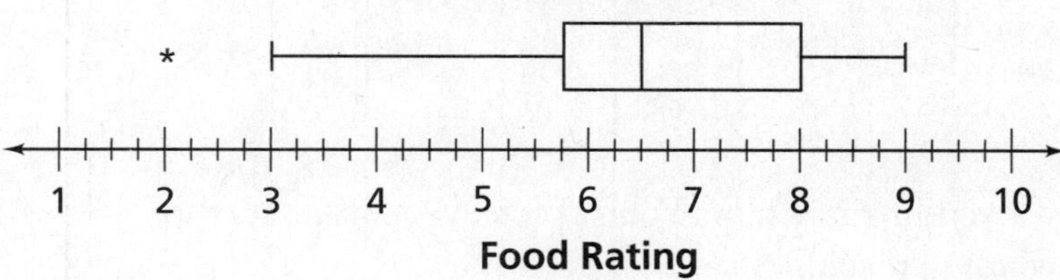

9. What is the range of students' ratings in the sample?

10. What percent of the students in the sample rated the cafeteria food between 5.75 and 9?

11. Based on the sample data, how many of the 1,000 students at the school do you estimate would rate the cafeteria food 6 or higher? Explain your reasoning.

12. A rating of 8 to 10 indicates "highly satisfied" on the rating scale.

a. What percent of students in the sample are "highly satisfied" with the cafeteria food?

b. Estimate how many students at the middle school would give the cafeteria food a "highly satisfied" rating.

Name ____________________ Date __________ Class __________

Skill: Random Samples

Investigation 2

Samples and Populations

You want to survey students in your school about their exercise habits. Tell whether Exercises 1–2 are likely to give a random sample of the population. Explain.

1. You select every tenth student on an alphabetical list of the students in your school. You survey the selected students in their first-period classes.

2. At lunchtime you stand by a vending machine. You survey every student who buys something from the vending machine.

In a mall, 2,146 shoppers (age 16 and older) were asked, "How often do you eat at a restaurant in the mall?" Here is how they responded.

3. What population does the sample represent?

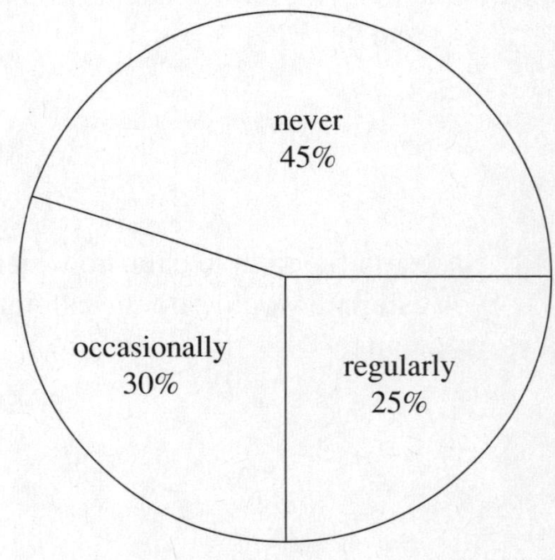

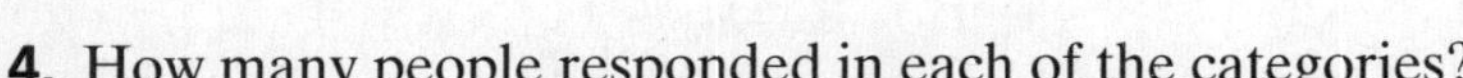

4. How many people responded in each of the categories?

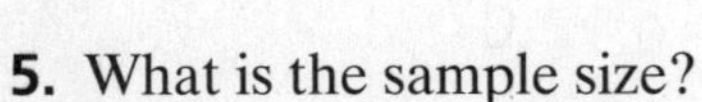

5. What is the sample size?

6. Can you tell if the sample is random?

Additional Practice

1. A group of students surveyed several pizza shops in two parts of the United States. They asked about prices and sizes of small, medium, and large cheese pizzas, and they made box plots from the data they collected.

   a. These box plots show the prices for each size pizza, including outliers. Which size appears to be the least expensive? Explain your reasoning.

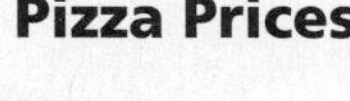

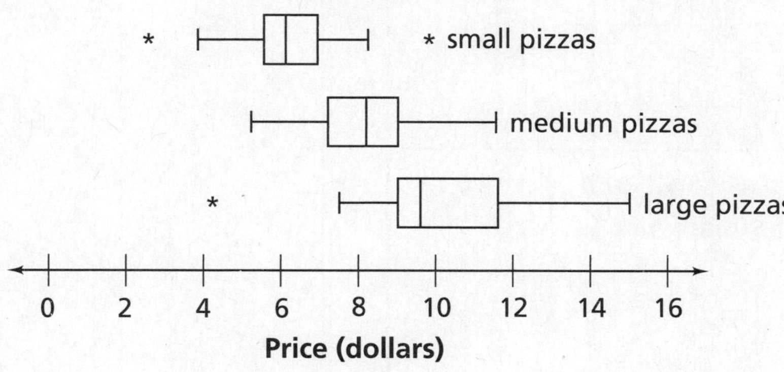

   b. One of the small pizzas had a diameter of 8 inches and a price of \$3.87. Its price per square inch is \$0.077. How was this calculated?

c. These box plots show the price per square inch of pizza for each size. Which size appears to be the best buy? Explain.

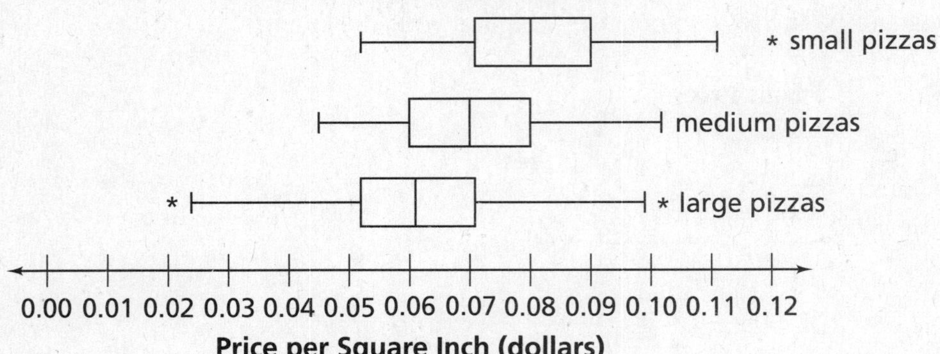

d. Consider your responses to parts (a) and (c). Which set of box plots better reflects the actual price of a pizza? Explain.

Additional Practice *(continued)*

2. Suppose Jeff and Ted decide to change their advertising slogan to "Seven giant chips in every cookie!" They mix 70 chips into a batch of dough and make 10 cookies from the dough. When they remove the cookies from the oven and inspect them, they count the number of chips in each cookie. Their results are shown below. Notice that only 5 of the 10 cookies contained 7 chips or more.

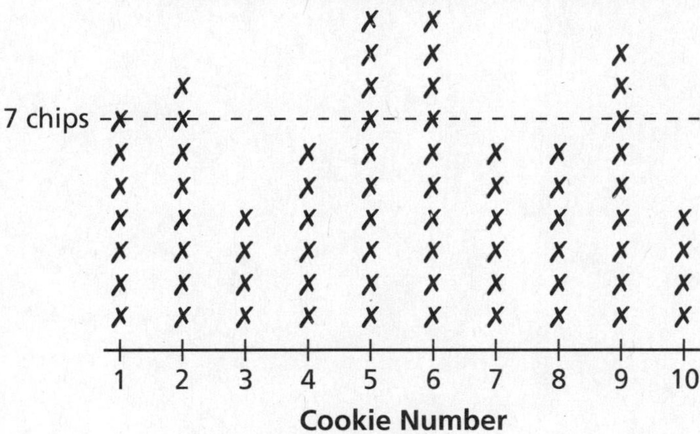

a. Conduct a simulation to determine the number of chips needed to be added to a batch of 10 cookies until each cookie has at least 7 chips. Carry out the simulation five times so that you have five data values for the number of chips needed.

b. What is the minimum number of chips Jeff and Ted should use to be confident that each cookie will have at least 7 chips? Support your answer with statistics and graphs.

3. After testing many samples, an egg shipper determined that approximately 3 in every 100 cartons of eggs will contain at least one cracked egg. The company ships 200,000 cartons of eggs every month. Estimate how many cartons of eggs each month will contain at least one cracked egg.

4. From a shipment of 500 batteries, a sample of 25 was selected at random and tested. If 2 batteries in the sample were found to be dead, how many dead batteries would be expected in the entire shipment?

Name ____________________ Date __________ Class __________

Skill: Simulation

Investigation 3

Samples and Populations

A soccer player scores a goal on about 1 out of every 6 shots.

1. Explain how you could use a number cube to simulate the player's scoring average.

2. Use your simulation to find the probability of the player making 4 out of 5 of her next attempts.

Name ______________________________ Date ____________ Class ____________

Additional Practice

Investigation 4

Samples and Populations

Use the tables below, which display the results of a study of 47 half-ounce boxes of two brands of raisins.

Vine Hill Raisins

Number in Box	Mass (grams)
29	14.78
35	16.59
35	16.01
35	16.55
36	16.99
38	16.34
38	16.3
39	17.83
39	16.66
39	18.36
39	16.93
40	16.25
40	17.92
40	17.12
40	17.37
42	16.95
42	17.45
44	18.48
35	15.64
36	16.88
36	16.36
36	16.3
37	17.25
37	15.61

Number in Box	Mass (grams)
38	16.3
38	16.85
38	17.33
38	17.57
40	16.2
40	16.78
40	17.35
41	17.43
41	16.64
41	16.62
31	14.7
34	16.04
35	16.81
36	16.86
36	16.75
36	17.18
36	15.77
36	16.28
37	16.25
37	17.42
37	16.25
37	15.63
37	17.74

Suntime Raisins

Number in Box	Mass (grams)
25	14.15
26	16.74
27	15.42
27	16.74
27	15.98
28	17.43
28	16.44
28	16.55
28	15.55
28	15.33
29	16.75
29	16.19
29	16.36
29	17.1
29	16.58
30	16.36
30	16.29
31	15.9
29	16.18
29	15.91
30	16.66
31	15.73
31	16.38
31	16.92

Number in Box	Mass (grams)
31	16.13
31	16.6
32	16.6
33	16.55
33	17.11
34	16.88
34	18.1
35	17.63
35	17.32
26	15.34
28	14.11
29	16.94
29	15.16
29	15.75
29	15.65
30	16.5
31	15.83
31	17.17
32	16.6
32	16.59
32	16.38
33	17.11
34	17.24

Additional Practice *(continued)*

1. The two scatter plots below show the data from the tables. Which scatter plot shows the data for Suntime raisins? Which shows the data for Vine Hill raisins? Explain your reasoning.

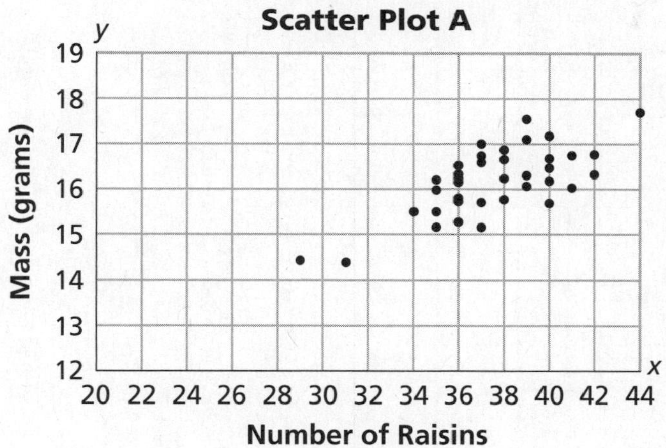

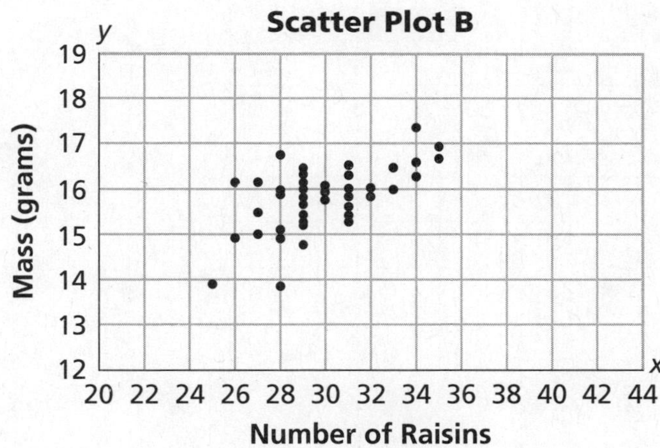

2. Is this statement true or false: "Vine Hill raisins typically have more raisins in a box than do Suntime raisins." Explain your reasoning using the two graphs.

3. Is there a relationship between the number of raisins in a box and the mass in grams? Explain.

Additional Practice *(continued)*

For Exercises 4–6, use the data below.

Chicken Sandwiches From Restaurant Chains

Size (oz)	Calories	Fat (g)	Carbohydrates (g)
8	360	7	44
10	370	8	53
8	380	4	57
9	400	5	57
8	400	16	37
8	470	20	51
8	470	20	46
10	500	24	52
8	510	19	57
10	540	30	42
9	550	23	55
10	550	30	46
10	570	25	48
12	580	19	58
11	640	29	61
13	660	29	56
12	720	30	65
13	740	30	78
12	910	40	86
15	950	56	76

4. a. Make a scatterplot for size vs. calories.

b. Describe any relationship you see between the size of the sandwich and calories. Explain your reasoning.

5. a. Make a scatterplot for size of sandwich vs. fat.

b. What is the relationship between sandwich size and fat content? Explain.

6. a. Make a scatterplot for size vs. carbohydrates.

b. What is the relationship between size of a sandwich and the carbohydrates? Explain.

Name ______________________ Date ____________ Class ____________

Additional Practice *(continued)*

7. a. Make a scatterplot of the data below for price vs. weight.

Bike Comparisons

Type of Bike	Price	Weight (lb)
Front Suspension Mountain Bike	$450	29.5
Front Suspension Mountain Bike	$440	29.5
Front Suspension Mountain Bike	$440	30.5
Front Suspension Mountain Bike	$450	31.5
Front Suspension Mountain Bike	$440	31.0
Front Suspension Mountain Bike	$500	30.5
Front Suspension Mountain Bike	$500	31.5
Front Suspension Mountain Bike	$400	32.0
Comfort Bike	$300	33.0
Comfort Bike	$300	32.5
Comfort Bike	$300	35.5
Comfort Bike	$300	32.0
Comfort Bike	$280	31.5
Comfort Bike	$290	33.0
Comfort Bike	$285	33.5

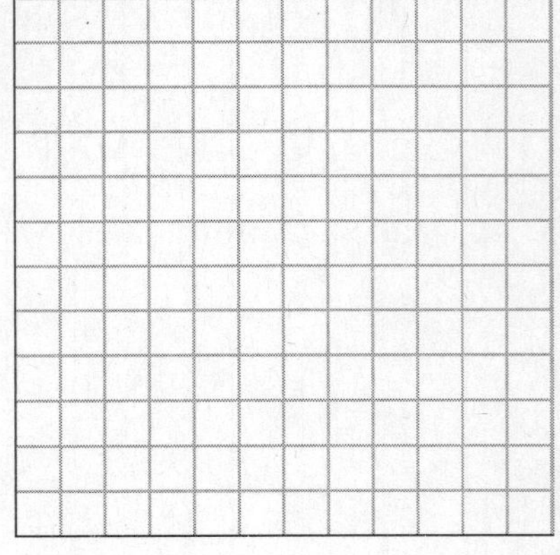

b. Is there a strong or weak relationship between the weight of a bike and the price for the bike? Explain your reasoning.

c. If you pay more, are likely to get a heavier or lighter bike?

Name ______________________ Date ____________ Class ____________

Skill: Scatter Plots

Investigation 4

Samples and Populations

1. Make a scatter plot showing the number of homeowners on one axis and vacation homeowners on the other axis. If there is a trend, draw a trend line.

Residents of Maintown		
Year	Homeowners	Vacation Homeowners
1997–98	2,050	973
1996–97	1,987	967
1995–96	1,948	1,041
1994–95	1,897	1,043
1993–94	1,862	1,125
1992–93	1,832	1,126

2. Make a scatter plot for the data. If there is a trend, draw a trend line.

Arm Span vs. Height		
Person #	Arm Span	Height
1	156	162
2	157	160
3	159	162
4	160	155
5	161	160
6	161	162
7	162	170
8	165	166
9	170	170
10	170	167
11	173	185
12	173	176

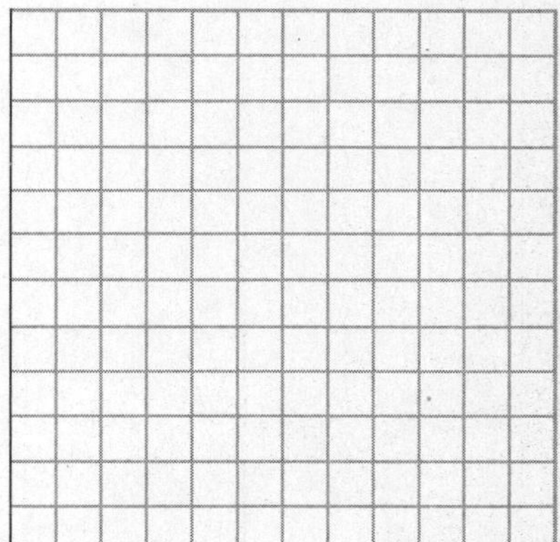

Skill: Scatter Plots *(continued)*

Decide whether the data in each scatter plot follow a linear pattern. If they do, find the equation of a trend line.

3.

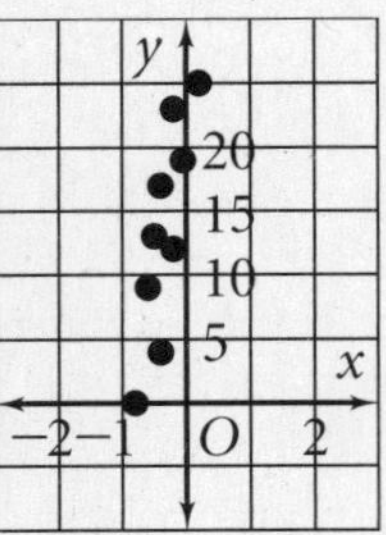

4.

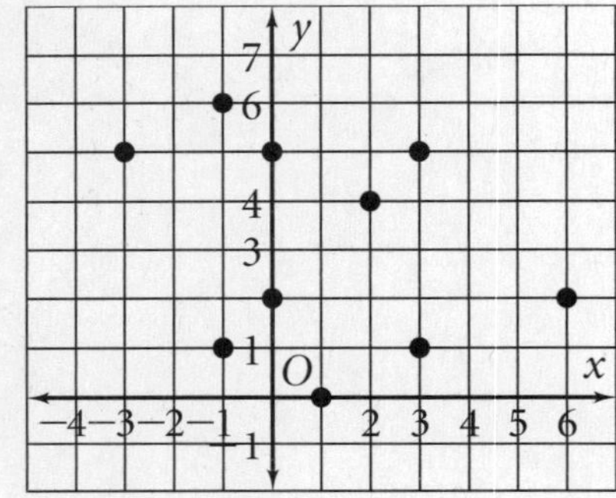

5.

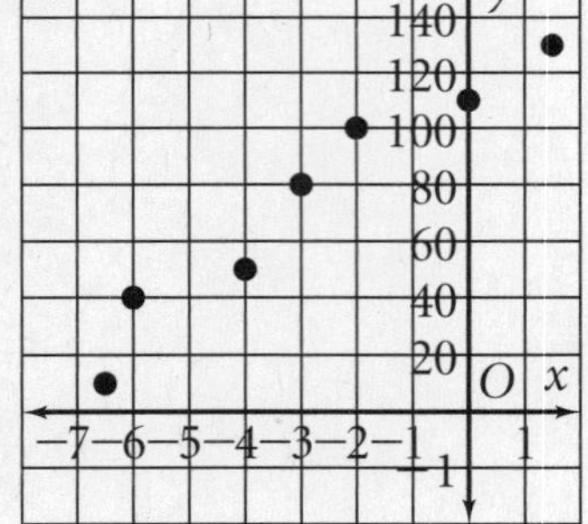